Recovering from a Position
of Ignorance

Recovering from a Position of Ignorance

John Wallis

ISBN 978-0-9572795-1-3

Preface

I have been encouraged by family and friends to share my recent personal experiences of 'complementary' solutions to medical conditions, in the hope they may benefit others. No intentionally false claims are offered but in my case, thankfully as of today, no progressive symptoms of Multiple Sclerosis have been observed since the months immediately following the condition being diagnosed. If anything, some but not all symptoms have been reversed. Perhaps it's my good fortune or a coincidence but improvements to my health and wellbeing have been clear for everyone to see since undertaking a month-long course of Ayurvedic treatment in 2009. There are no guarantees that the improvements made will be maintained indefinitely but all the time I'm feeling much stronger and able, the greater is my belief. In my opinion, this is definitely not the solution for everyone, especially the faint-hearted but if nothing else, hopefully parts of the following account will be mildly amusing, even for the cynics.

Although I have no problem making fun of myself, it is certainly not my intention to expose my hosts, fellow patients or their families to ridicule. The following includes a close-up account of time spent at an Ayurvedic hospital in Southern India and in no way reflects the thoughts and opinions of others. I apologise if some of my naive observations cause offence but please bear in mind that I am still in the process of recovering from a position of ignorance.

Stress, what stress?

In a perverse way, diagnosis came as a relief, to me if not to Joanie and the family. I had been aware that something was not quite right for a number of years but was unable to link it with any one thing in particular. Everyone gets tired sometimes don't they, especially when working hard and under stress? And what's the problem with stress anyway? I had thrived on it for years, enjoying the buzz of an adrenalin rush and kept striving for more satisfaction from my efforts.

Times change, however and so do people, their priorities and their coping mechanisms. Well that was me prior to engineering my own redundancy and then subsequently, while trying to find enough work to keep us afloat financially and hold my dignity intact. Despite the high salary and supportive noises from senior management, in my cluttered head, my career seemed to be spiralling out of control and frankly, I wasn't coping too well with the 'symptoms'.

When under pressure, the mind can perform unpleasant tricks on the body, leading you to consider all manner of illnesses and that's exactly what happened. I had never been a fully-fledged hypochondriac, other than experiencing annual bouts of 'man flu' but I was starting to doubt my ability to find logical solutions for my condition, especially when the medical profession seems to put everything down to stress, which most people encounter in all walks of life. But perhaps it was stress and if so, I was proving singularly unsuccessful at dissipating it.

Falling over in the street for no apparent reason is difficult to accept, especially as it was happening all too frequently and ruining both the knees of my trousers and what was left of my self-esteem. It was embarrassing and painful, as I behaved like a sad but harmless village drunk, without the benefits of alcohol consumption.

I was tired the whole time, needing frequent naps, as well as long bouts of sleep at night. And the waterworks weren't as efficient as in my younger years, my diminishing bladder control frightening me into anticipating the onset of dementia.

Ultimately, we turned to the medical profession for advice and assistance. Lower back pains were put down to lack of exercise and too much inter-continental air travel in cramped economy class seats, while numbness in the left leg was probably the result of a trapped nerve. A loss of control in my writing hand had to be caused by stress because there was no evidence of a stroke and as for the constant fatigue, well obviously you need more exercise and should cut down on the stress levels.

After all, I was in my late 40s (*but felt older*), seldom exercised (*all fitness clubs and swimming are boring*), ate badly (*still love the idea of grazing on ice cream and chocolate*), had smoked heavily for 25 years (*miss that heady sensation when lighting up*), drank more caffeine and alcohol than recommended, worked too many hours, as well as worrying about holding on to my job and maintaining a comfortable standard of living.

There was nothing abnormal about my situation; everything could be put down to stress and bad living. It all seemed entirely logical and plausible… up to a point. The problem was, whatever conventional remedial actions we took made no difference. Exercise, for example, made me more tired and ache, while giving up smoking and caffeine had simply made me more irritable!

In my 20s and 30s, work had been very fulfilling but through no fault of my first wife, my personal life had lost energy and meaning. Subsequently, with Joanie, the tables had turned completely. Now, a wonderfully happy private life was mismatched with a sterile and frustrating work existence. So I gave up the well-paid job that caused me so much internal angst and after an initial period of calm, began to stress about how I was to earn a crust and fill the yawning gap left in my life.

Coming to terms with MS

The final, all-important piece in the MS jigsaw fell into place in early 2006, almost two years after I had left full-time employment and struggled unsuccessfully to develop an alternative career. Money was tight but thankfully, a couple of regular consultancy jobs contributed to keeping the household afloat. We had moved into a bungalow in need of thorough modernisation, giving me a challenge to get my teeth into. Considering the limited budget available, the end result was very satisfying.

I remember that February morning vividly, awakening with a hideous pain around the right eye and a partial loss of vision, akin to looking through a grubby net curtain. Almost three years earlier, I had 'treated' myself to laser surgery on both eyes. Subsequently, some of the immediate sight improvements had been lost and the ongoing paranoia led me to believe that a serious malfunction had occurred.

It had all started so positively. Having worn glasses the thickness of bottle bases since the age of 15, it was so liberating to wake up and see the time without the aid of lenses. No more cleaning smudged finger prints, the freedom to swim and snorkel unaided and no infuriating misting up when entering a hot room from the cold outside. Sadly, the full benefits of 20:20 vision haven't been maintained subsequently, although the result is still so much better than before.

With the pain and reduced vision in the right eye came colour blindness and the depressing if unsubstantiated conclusion that it all related to the laser eye surgery. Having been bollocked by an unfriendly GP for undertaking laser treatment in the first place *("if it was safe, don't you think surgeons and opticians would have stopped wearing glasses?")*, I took myself to a local ophthalmologist for an emergency examination with all manner of wizzy gadgets and equipment.

My mood and confidence weren't exactly improved when sent to an eye specialist at East Surrey Hospital with possible optic neuritis, especially when I didn't have the foggiest idea what the diagnosis meant. Ten minutes of simple research on the internet put me straight, as we began coming to terms with the probability that at the ripe old age of 49, I had Multiple Sclerosis.

Complaints may persist about patient care levels within the UK National Health Service but within 14 days, an MRI scan was arranged and shortly thereafter, Joanie and I were sitting in front of the Neurology Consultant at East Surrey Hospital, being told he was 99% certain that it was MS. When asked about the remaining 1%, he gave me the opportunity to participate in a lumber puncture, a generous offer that I declined, on the grounds it would merely prove the inevitable and would definitely hurt!

According to the statistics, I was entirely the wrong profile in terms of age, while the majority of sufferers are female. How could this diagnosis be correct? Misguidedly, I thought it made a difference that there was no history of MS in the family and in every other respect, I was relatively healthy. And yet, when the doctor presented me with a list of symptoms, I ticked just about every box and in some instances, had done so for a number of years.

I saw the same doctor three times in the space of 12 months and I haven't been to see him since. He arranged a series of six specialist physiotherapy sessions that began the process of improving my physical flexibility but apart from initially offering a short course of steroids to reduce the swelling in my brain, it was clear there was very little he could do for me. My GP was also very supportive (a different one from she who unjustifiably had chastised me about laser eye treatment) but ultimately, I was left with the stark option of wallowing in self-pity or simply getting on with life. In truth, the family ensured that self-pity wasn't an option, while a telephone conversation with a lady from the local MS Society helpline served to reinforce my desire not to let these stupid symptoms consume me. Joanie had heard about a yoga teacher nearby, providing tuition to people like me who, thankfully, were still comparatively mobile. In the course of conversation, the MS Society helpline suggested I was in denial, I should accept my condition and find out via their meetings and literature how others deal with it.

However well meaning, that single comment galvanised me to explore alternative solutions and find one or more that could improve my situation. Don't get me wrong, I could be miserable as sin at times, angry about this latest misfortune that knocked us back again and generally feeling outrageously sorry for myself. In addition, the reactions generated among family, friends and work colleagues, especially when approaching them with a walking stick to mask the limp, were often extreme, to say the least. There was embarrassment, some horror, discomfort and a fair amount of pity, combined with a general sense of disbelief. It was by no means at the "Does he take sugar" level but when attending trade shows for example, I was generously provided with more opportunities to take the weight off my feet and a drink or two than ever before. It's always said at such times that you discover who your real friends are and that was certainly the case for me.

Considering alternative solutions

Have you tried explaining to an employer your need for regular naps during working hours, your ability to carry only the lightest laptop computer when travelling, your need for a desk as close as possible to the loo and your inability to climb stairs without difficulty? Never having encountered the condition before, I can imagine the initial concern that I wasn't simply pulling a fast one for an easy life. Thankfully, through most of this period, I was fortunate to remain self-employed, providing the flexibility required to continue working at times and places that took account of my physical limitations.

Sometimes, I still pushed the boundaries too far but soon learnt to respect those boundaries. It hurt my pride to give up the sporty car with its manual transmission but an automatic gearbox meant I could continue driving up and down the UK and on a couple of occasions, into mainland Europe. Similarly, a battery-powered razor and electric toothbrush simplified bathroom ablutions. Sadly, the condition also meant I could no longer perform such household chores as ironing and vacuuming the carpets but then again, we all have to make sacrifices at different times! More seriously, although it was much less stressful, I hadn't been used to the mind numbing sub-editing work I was now expected to enjoy for many, many years. I had been used to generating the ideas and pulling the strings to make them happen and it was hard coming to terms with shovelling everyone else's debris again.

Putting my ego and reduced earning potential to one side, however, at least self-employment provided the opportunity to arrange convenient appointments with a variety of complementary practitioners around South East England. Although I was able to continue working, after a few months, it was proving to be both physically and mentally debilitating. We needed to find ways to boost energy levels and keep the body's muscles as active and toned as possible. Regular visits to the gym, cycle rides, road running etc were out of the question. Such activities simply drained me of energy within seconds and my lack of co-ordination became severely exposed.

It genuinely helps when your wife is a fully qualified aromatherapist / reflexoligist / kinesiologist and can provide regular treatments but on its own, this was not the answer. She also works full-time and the last thing we needed was for Joanie to become ill as well, so we tried a number of other therapies, some relatively sensible and others, completely wacky, until we found something that worked.

I had already been converted to the benefits of homeopathy, Joanie having persuaded me to see Adrian Brito-Babapulle about a longstanding issue with a hiatus hernia and interminable bouts of sneezing more than a decade ago. Several doctors had tried and failed to solve either problem with drugs but Adrian managed to clear them both up. He is an extremely intelligent and infuriatingly intuitive person. Coming from totally different positions, Adrian and I are equally stubborn and confident in our beliefs, except mine when it comes to complementary therapies. He has been known to sigh and rebuke me for failing to follow his line of thought and let my body express what is best for me. This is a totally alien concept for those of us that are mere mortals and I have told him so. In defence of my position, I explained that when my wife takes the car to the garage with a problem, she does so in total ignorance of the workings of the internal combustion engine. Instead, she employs the services of a specialist to identify the problem and find a solution.

That's how I view the role of homeopaths, doctors etc. Or should I say, that's how I previously viewed it. Today, I recognise that I share a responsibility for the state of my body and mind and should also play a more proactive role in the identification and implementation of appropriate treatments. Call it belief, willpower or intuition, it's my problem and I no longer wish to be led by the nose to do what's apparently 'best for me' or simply give up because no single magic pill has been developed as a cure.

In co-ordination with Joanie's massage therapies, we were managing to halt the onset of further MS symptoms but my mobility, flexibility and the constant fatigue had not improved to any great extent. A series of sessions with a local chiropractor brought temporary pain relief to my lower back and left leg, while an internationally acknowledged healer in Central London was successful in boosting my energy levels, sending what can only be described as charges of electricity through my body. At the time, the cynic in me found it difficult to acknowledge that Seka was making a difference but that seemed to be the case. Unfortunately, her treatment sessions were simultaneously draining our financial resources, requiring us to find another, more cost-effective solution. Other Reiki practitioners were consulted, with varying degrees of success and at one point, I saw a well-meaning individual in Surrey, who 'talked' to my 'medical team' and worked with them to repair me. Let's just say that we didn't share too many consultations!

The Ayurvedic option

It was a dubious birthday present, one that didn't really appeal to me but equally, I recognised that it was important to Joanie. She had identified a residential introduction to Ayurvedic medicines, treatments and philosophies, held in Camberley and run by a Sri Lankan businessman and his wife. He was a fairly recent convert, having benefited personally from treatments in South Asia.

Joanie believed this ancient form of Indian healthcare merited closer evaluation and I was prepared to give it a go. Frankly, what did I have to lose? Over the course of the weekend, we discussed some of the basic principles of Ayurveda, the associated therapies and vegetarian foods of southern India, as well as the benefits of healthier living generally. This included a series of yoga and meditation sessions, a massage treatment and a consultation with an Ayurvedic doctor.

In all honesty, most of the programme and our fellow (all female) participants left me cold. This wasn't a romantic weekend for two in the Surrey countryside. I wasn't too enamoured with the food, couldn't do most of the yoga exercises and lacked the focus/interest in the meditation. Dr Stephen intrigued me, however. He came across as a very caring and intuitive person and could obviously see my discomfort, both in my immediate surroundings and because of the symptoms I was experiencing.

He practiced Ayurvedic medicine in West London and was happy to treat me there if I wished. It was clear, however, that an hour long massage every month in the UK would be insufficient to make a meaningful difference. There were simply too many distractions in daily western life. Following a lengthy pause, Dr Stephen, who studied Ayurvedic medicine in his home state of Kerala, in the South West of India, posed a simple but poignant question: "How serious are you about addressing your condition?"

Little did I know what I was letting myself in for at the time but obviously, I expressed sufficient commitment for the doctor to recommend contacting a specialist Ayurvedic hospital in Kerala to ask if they would accept me as a patient. Located on the edge of the lush green village of Kottakkal in Malappuram District, Arya Vaidya Sala Kottakkal (AVS) is a charitable institution, engaged in the practice and propagation of Ayurveda.

Established in 1902 by the physician and philanthropist Vaidyaratnam P S Varier, AVS is thought to have been the first facility where all classic panchakarma and specialist Kerala therapies were made available to patients in an organised way, under the umbrella of a modern hospital. The memory of Dr Varier is clearly held in high esteem, his framed image hanging from the walls of every room at the Kottakkal hospital.

Three manufacturing units produce more than 550 different Ayurvedic medicines, while research initiatives are undertaken on-site. AVS operates Ayurvedic hospitals in Kottakkal, Delhi, Kochin and Aluva and has its own herbal gardens.

In essence, the treatments provided are said to constitute an effective combination for the radical cure/management of many 'diseases'. According to AVS literature, these methods of purification (sodhana) and pecification (samana) remove the cause of morbidity from the body and pacify the impact of morbidity.

All of this meant absolutely nothing to me when, like a lamb to the slaughter, I emailed the hospital doctors and asked if they could help. I took courage from feedback received from reliable Indian business contacts that there was no better source of Ayurvedic treatment and in September 2009, set out on the adventure of a lifetime. Fun it most definitely was not but what a difference the experience was to make to my health and wellbeing.

Confronting life-long prejudices

To be brutally frank, when growing up as a child, India held little fascination for me. A stereotypical Anglo Saxon upbringing led me to believe the place to be dirty and the people poor and exploited, with low standards of hygiene and education. The food would be too hot and spicy for my palate and the country was full of disease and inequality. In my experience, there is more than a grain of truth in many of these prejudiced beliefs but the changes made in recent years are considerable and ongoing, changes both in Indian Society and my personal interpretations of it.

Like many from the suburban South East of England, throughout my school years in the 1960s and 70s, I never encountered anyone who had migrated from the sub-continent. In my later teenage years, I vaguely recall alcohol-induced visits to Indian restaurants but such establishments were still few and far between in Surrey. Even had I been sufficiently sober to talk coherently to the waiters, many had been born and bred in the UK and as direct links to any mother country fade, family memories can become increasingly nostalgic and inaccurate.

There has long been a massive chasm between the few extremely rich and the many very poor. Less than two decades ago, India's affluent middle classes accounted for a meagre 10% of the nation's population but stop to consider the numbers involved and already, this represented more than 10 million people. Today, as the country's economy expands apace, the amount of disposable income also increases, creating new wealth, aspirations and expectations.

I am embarrassed to admit that I railed against the prospect of visiting for many years and when eventually I conceded, I vowed that the experience need never be repeated. How wrong can you be? In a publishing and exhibitions management career that has spanned more than 35 years, I've probably spent more time in India than any other country outside the UK. It has to be emphasised, however, that until now, most of my experiences have been undertaken in short doses of a few days, in a luxurious and pampered bubble.

My sensitive stomach and I have been sick in some of the world's finest hotels over the years. I became an expert on the intricacies of bathroom sanitary systems, inspecting toilet bowls at close quarters. For my first exciting and challenging business trip beyond the relatively comfortable environments of Western Europe and North America, I arranged a hectic14 day tour of South East Asia, interviewing relevant business leaders in five countries. Even today, the opportunity to visit such places as Bangkok, Kuala Lumpur, Jakarta, Manila and Singapore represents a fantastic opportunity but during the early 1980s, these were still faraway places that few were lucky enough to see at close quarters.

As an ambitious 26 year old, I embraced the challenge, pushing myself to maximise every minute of every day. It could be exhausting yet stimulating, mentally as well as physically. Although cautious and suspicious by nature, I sometimes found myself in potentially dangerous and compromising positions, mostly the result of my own stupidity. Retrospectively, the ignorance of youth saw me through these awkward situations and ultimately, I was perhaps fortunate to have avoided compromising personal safety.

My highly sensitive stomach was less fortunate, reacting violently to different foods, temperature changes and the stressful situations encountered. I had never been a great lover of fish but sit me closer than 5ft from a red snapper let alone a lobster and I could vomit for my country. And in Thailand or Indonesia especially, it was virtually impossible to avoid seafood at that time. Even after confirming with restaurants that the meal ordered was definitely chicken or beef, I could be crouched over a friendly toilet bowl four hours later, almost to the second. It took me more than a decade to realise that fish paste is the starting point for most cooking in the region and that basically, I didn't stand a chance.

From the outset, even the most carefully planned meals were disastrous. Months before arriving in Jakarta, advice was taken from a senior colleague who had been the company's first to visit the city a few weeks earlier. He recommended a safe, if outrageously expensive, hotel and a menu that had seen his digestive system through the experience unscathed. His mantra was to avoid the water, salad, fruit and vegetables at all costs, order well done steaks from the hotel restaurant and drink plenty of beer. Knowing no better – after all, this was a director with years of international travel under his belt – I followed his advice to the letter… and was hideously sick for the next two days, while continuing to work.

Thankfully, my next stop was Singapore, a haven of peace and tranquillity in which to recover from the uncertainties and anguish presented in the days prior by Manila, Surabaya and Jakarta. Subsequently, I grew to cope with all three cities, as I learnt to understand their different cultures, while meeting and developing local contacts. Arriving at Changi Airport for the first time however, I could almost feel the stresses and strains melt away. For the first time since leaving the UK, I took a taxi, confident in the belief that I was guaranteed to reach my destination without being ripped off and with all of my possessions. Most of the dangers had been in my head of course but that's not much comfort at the time when you're alone and making it up as you go along.

On a positive note, there wasn't an ounce of fat on me at this time, with a stomach as flat as an ironing board. Less helpful was an increasing intolerance to many foods, combined with the creation of my very own hiatus hernia. The condition was controlled for too long by a concoction of mild drugs, designed to restrict the stomach's acidic fluids from refluxing into the throat. Only later did I discover the prognosis that some of the medication could lie in the bottom of the stomach for years, like a corrosive nuclear waste material, dumped in your personal back yard.

On that first Indian adventure, in 1993, I was escorted around Mumbai, New Delhi and several rural towns in Haryana and Uttar Pradesh, where the greatest density of India's glassmakers were based. To the best of my knowledge, I was among the first of the company's Editors to undertake such an exotic and extensive trip, which involved conducting detailed interviews with 23 of the industry's leading personalities in the space of five days. It was a punishing and stressful schedule, made worse by the fact that 36 hours before my planned arrival in Mumbai, a series of terrorist bombs ripped through the city's main business district. Thankfully, unlike the orchestrated attacks that killed so many people in Mumbai in 2008, the perpetrators were not as well organised or as deadly. In 1993, however, we didn't have wall-to-wall television news coverage either to boost or deflate confidence, requiring us to place immense faith in my hosts for my safety.

My Sales Manager was a major influence in deciding to undertake that first trip. Working on a business magazine for the international glassmaking industry, every summer Geoff and I would wrangle for weeks over editorial feature ideas for the following year. As Editor, I was in the enviable position of visiting glassmakers around the world, interviewing them and writing features about their businesses. Geoff and some of India's leading industrialists had canvassed for my attendance for several years but I had been resistant.

The 1980s and early 1990s represented a period of major growth for the industry in many countries. There was so much to talk about in Europe, North and Latin America, the Middle East and especially South East Asia. India at this time was a closed market economy, with limited opportunity for the importation of western equipment and negligible foreign investment potential. So why subject myself to the discomforts of the sub-continent for so little return when other, more dynamic markets beckoned? What's more, how would my sensitive stomach survive?

Subsequently of course, India has emerged as one of world's major growth economies and my initial negativity was proved to be totally misguided. For almost two decades, I was fortunate to witness and report on many of the business and social changes, counting some of the local glassmakers and suppliers among my friends. I was even more fortunate to explore the country and stay at some of its top hotels at someone else's expense! Cosseted in five star luxury, you are protected from the squalor faced by so many people in their day-to-day lives.

Although I say it myself, some very useful editorial copy came from those trips, together with a series of valuable trade shows. I have been lucky to gain the confidence and I hope, the respect of many enterprising local industrialists, some of whom provided comforting advice in the build-up to my Kerala adventure.

How very different my latest trip to India would be. Apart from the novelty of financing the month long experience, I would be staying in very different conditions, in a part of the country that was completely new to me, alone among people I didn't know and with a frustrating medical condition that I needed to address via techniques that were alien to me.

Treatment types

The following abridged daily accounts are taken from a diary, maintained during my stay in September 2009 and emailed home. Based largely on the naive observations of an Englishman who was completely out of his comfort zone, they were intended to be as lighthearted as my mood would allow, to maintain the spirits of everyone at home, as well as my own.

Effectively, three different types of massage treatment were received over the course of 28 days, geared primarily to stimulate the neurological system. I didn't know the names of these treatments at the time or what precisely was going on around me, hence the descriptions of 'baking trays', 'polishing' etc.

The first, Dhara, involves the liberal application of medicated oil to the head and body, while lying on a specially-made 'table', or as I referred to it, 'basting tray'. The oil is made to drop gently and continuously onto the forehead via an ingenious device for an hour and is massaged into the scalp.

Dhara was performed in combination with Pizhichil and is considered particularly effective for neurological disorders (eg Multiple Sclerosis) and psychosomatic conditions.

A Malayalam term, Pizhichil literally means 'squeezing'. To be precise, pieces of cloth dipped in warm medicated oil are squeezed over the body in a rhythmic manner. As the warm oil spreads over the body, trained masseurs provide what is described as a gentle massage, although I would dispute the use of the word 'gentle'. Pizhichil is considered particularly effective in the treatment of inflammatory joint diseases, disease of bones, obstructive pulmonary disorders, diseases that affect muscles and their rejuvination.

The third treatment received, Navarakizhi is a procedure in which the body is massaged with warm and wet boiled Navara rice bags. The rice is cooked in a combination of milk and herbs to make up the bags, which are rubbed over the body. This procedure is used to treat a wide variety of conditions, everything from cerebral palsy and polio myelitis to degenerative diseases.

In the three years since my initial treatments, the hospital has become much better at the art of communication, explaining these treatments to prospective patients in simple yet effective illustrated leaflets. In 2009, however, much less background information was available, leaving the minds of many patients (including mine) to devise some fairly ridiculous and embarrassingly simplistic descriptions, as the following detailed exerts confirm.

Dhara involves the liberal application of warm, medicated oil to the head and body. Not only is the process sticky and smelly but washing the oil from the scalp is not recommended for at least three days (Image courtesy of Arya Vaidya Sala Kottakkal).

Home, sweet home

Oh dear! Having experienced many of India's multi-cultural facets over the years, I had limited expectations of the hospital and as such, I cannot claim to have been surprised. There is something endearingly scruffy about India, a characteristic shared by all but the country's very best hotels. It's like the Charles Shultz character Pigpen in *Peanuts*; however hard people try to smarten him up, Pigpen always looks like he's been dragged through a hedge backwards. For the record, I like Pigpen and over the years, India has grown on me too.

Yes many places are undeniably dirty but this was definitely not the problem here. It is more that I was resident in a hospital, where the decor is sterile, what little furniture there is doesn't match and the stark lighting was acquired third-hand from a 1960's KGB torture facility.

Visualise dirty finger prints on the off-white walls, scruffy toilet bowl, seat and sink and the picture should be getting clearer. Add to this a corner of the bathroom that trendy Europeans like to call a 'wet room', complete with luke warm water and the image is almost there, other than a rock hard bed and the bulky padlock and bolts that adorn all guest room doors. *Subsequently, it has to be said, the showers were wonderfully hot, throughout the days and nights. Furthermore, a cleaner would sweep and disinfect the floor every morning.*

Basic is the term that most closely reflects my bedroom. I quickly discovered that a family-sized refrigerator was included in the price but not a television, which cost approximately 50 pence per day to hire. Guests need to bring their own bathroom towels and loo rolls as well unless, like me, you buy two towels from a shop down the road, along with some fragrant smelling tissues!

That worn out and dirty look was also found in the euphemistically called 'internet cafe'. This was hidden away in the basement of the hospital's main administration building and boasted some of the grubbiest and aged computer equipment I've seen for at least two decades. Not to put too fine a point on it, the furniture and especially the chairs were filthy. Thankfully, having brought my own laptop, I was able to connect into the internet cafe's system, paying a cash amount for use on a day-to-day basis. Even more thankfully, subsequently, Wi-Fi has been made available to all guest rooms and the internet café has been moved to a better location.

Anyone for spit roast?

Having talked with two doctors during the first morning, I waited patiently for a telephone call to confirm the time of my first treatment. When we reached the late afternoon with no message, I decided that my need for fragrant loo paper was too great and set off for the shops to buy some. I then enjoyed the decadence of my acquisition, followed by a shower.

Treatments take place from early morning and the last of the day starts at 15.30 so with no news received by 15.45, I thought I was utilising my time with admirable efficiency. Stupidly I forgot, this is India, where the locals love to please and surprise their guests in equal measure. So literally within seconds of partially drying with a newly acquired fluffy towel, one of my therapists knocked on the twice bolted door to confirm they were working late, especially for me!

I stress that only one of my therapists came to collect me, for there were six in total, all strong and fit young men. Pride and dignity desert you when you're helped on with a skimpy nappy and positioned on a large baking tray, complete with sides, presumably to stop guests from sliding out and to the floor as a means of escape.

Now I have a closer idea how a spit roast pig or a roast turkey must feel, thankfully without the sensation of sage and onion stuffing. It certainly felt like my giblets were being closely examined and the quantity of oils ensured I was well basted at all times with a sickly smelling concoction.

The therapy seemed to go on for an eternity but actually lasted an hour, as one person controlled the constant dribble of warm oil from a hanging reservoir, down a sisal rope and onto my forehead. One of his colleagues prevented the oil from rushing into my eyes with the aid of a wound linen Alice band and instead, worked it skilfully into my sodden scalp. Using a different oil, the other four pummelled my chest, stomach, arms and legs, forcing the cocktail through my body and onto the drip tray beneath; at least, that's how it felt to the 'patient'.

Halfway through the ordeal, I was asked if I was in any pain but by that time, I was almost completely numb and at less than my coherent best, nappy and all!

The indignity concluded with towelling down on my tray, before being lifted by arms and legs back onto the floor to dress. Undignified or what! Finally, a smidgeon of pungent powder is rubbed into the scalp, with a pinch sniffed up the nose, apparently to restrict the onset of a cold.

Back in my room, I was allowed to shower 60 minutes later, using a foul smelling green vegetable powder mixture which, when diluted in water, looked like soggy suet dumplings, filled with parsley or thyme and ready for roasting. Unfortunately, my head cannot be washed for three days at least, so I'm considering entering an Argentine Tango competition, where my slicked back hair looks the part even if the dance steps are missing.

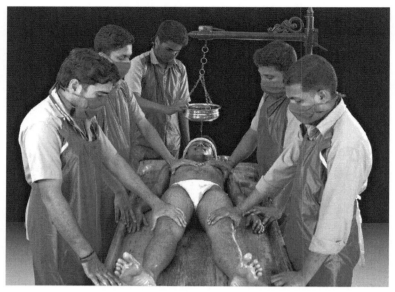

Personal dignity is lost when you're helped on with a skimpy nappy and massaged by six men on a large baking tray for 60 minutes. PS My baking tray and the attendants' clothing were not as smart as that shown here. Furthermore, there were no face masks and my nappy was considerably less conservative! (Image courtesy of Arya Vaidya Sala Kottakkal).

Consumption in ignorance

An important part of my daily routine involves taking various pungent tablets, syrups and pastes, all made at the hospital's own pharmacy. Trust is a key aspect of being a patient here, for I have zero knowledge of these medications, their constituents or likely outcomes, other than the fact that they smell disgusting, as do I no doubt!

Food produced in the hospital canteen is considerably more palatable and extremely cheap. Everything is vegetarian, very little on the menu appears to be too hot or spicy and my experience thus far is very positive. On Day One, I ate a bowl of sweet corn soup, plus basmati rice and vegetable korma. Add a fruit juice and a large bottle of water and the total bill comes to less than £2.

For breakfast on Day Two, a large bowl of porridge was washed down by a cup of sweet tea, costing under £1. A brief conversation with a second-time German patient has pointed me in the direction of my lunch selection. So far, my tummy is behaving itself and long may it continue.

Patience is key for patients

Having consumed breakfast before 08.00, I am now back in my room, awaiting the doctor's rounds before 10.00, to be followed by another treatment at some undetermined time during the day. I keep forgetting this is a hospital and not a health spa. As such, my function as a patient is to be patient, to recuperate and do what I'm not told. The doctor visited at 09.00, asked if everything was OK and left within 60 seconds. Brief and to the point but an interesting diversion for the brain dead nonetheless.

Not that there's much to do outside the four walls of my cell/room anyway. There is a small but beautifully maintained garden, which can be accessed at certain times of morning and early evening only, the internet room and a library. Rooms are located in five multi-story buildings and apart from the canteen, there are no communal lounges or areas to discuss escape plans with fellow inmates. I'm located on the sixth floor of Centenary Block and my treatments take place in rooms on the same level. There are two hour long yoga sessions daily but I haven't investigated these yet.

The town of Kottakkal looks to be fairly small, surrounded by lush vegetation. Weather conditions in early September are excellent, not too hot, with heavy rain on both mornings so far.

I've just seen Muhammad Ali on the CNN News Channel, pretending to spar with a much more agile Henry Cooper. Having emerged from my second encounter with six torturers, I'd rather face Ali in all his pomp. At least there's a knockout blow onto a bouncy floor before I get paid for turning up.

These guys are different from the first group of aggressors, including a chubby one in charge of the swinging oil container. They manage to generate the same degree of pain in my feet but laugh while doing so. My first encounter with a death squad left no residual pain and I slept unhindered that night. This time, my muscles ache – yes both of them, simultaneously – and I desperately needed a two hour nap to recover.

Six hours later, showered and refreshed, I'm ready for a gourmet meal... and tea. That's it for now. Back tomorrow for the next encounter with the devil's disciples and their torture table, which is constructed from glass fibre by the way, rather than metal. So much more hygienic, don't you agree?

Cocktails on prescription

Slept fitfully through the night, rising at 07.00 for porridge and tea. Most inmates order room service but unless I visit the canteen on a regular basis, my social life will be severely compromised.

The doctor visited for two minutes at 08.20 and prescribed medicated water, to be taken along with the cocktail of vegetable-based pills and potions. One is a sticky paste, with the consistency, smell and taste of road tar but minus the bubbles I recall from childhood hot summers. Sadly, one teaspoon each day is all I'm allowed to take.

Really not looking forward to today's treatment. Aching and very sore from the previous two sessions. On a more positive note, get it out of the way and I should be able to wash my hair within 24 hours.

One more thing and don't get carried away but the split in my left big toe... has almost disappeared!

Third treatment concluded without major incident or pain but disappointed to report that the recession must have finally infiltrated this backwater of Kerala. Instead of six attendants, I have just four today. Either standards are slipping or they are getting busier.

Apparently, there are 400 attendants at the hospital (200 male, 200 female) and they're kept busy treating people for a wide variety of complaints, from cancer to back pains, diabetes to RSI. They follow instructions laid down by the doctors, mechanics following a manual rather than fully empowered therapists, interpreting a need.

I feel much lighter and less pained today. After 60 minutes of rest, I am allowed to visit the internet cafe. My only disappointment is that the doctor has to confirm whether I can wash my hair tomorrow and it's sod's law that I'll be last on his list. Patience, patience!

First signs of frustration

I managed to sleep even less last night. Thank God for the US Open tennis on the TV through the night! I wish there was somewhere more comfortable to read and use the laptop. The 'desktop' is too high for the plastic garden chair and the bed is even more uncomfortable. Today, I will ask again about the possibility of a suite, not just for the extra comfort but also for the internet access. Please let one become available in the coming days.

It's frightening how reliant Society has become on internet technology and how frustrating it is, either when broadband is restricted or missing altogether. Was not at all happy Thursday evening in the internet cafe when the mouse had a life of its own and needed a bloody good clean. My first sign of frustration in four challenging days!

Mixed up my diet yesterday, starting with porridge for breakfast, a toasted cheese sandwich for lunch which was cold and bore no relation to anything I've eaten before and vegetable noodles for dinner. If this description doesn't tell you how boring my life has become, nothing will. However, I'm becoming slimmer by the minute, both as a result of the limited diet and the daily pummelling by my tormentors. I now have a full set of ribs on view when I stretch, my man boobs are shrinking and my pot belly is threatening to leave me for someone more caring and understanding. Furthermore, I may not have much access to the sun but I am becoming darker, thanks largely to the treacle-coloured oils.

I'm struggling to remain positive this morning, especially after my latest 60 seconds visit from the doctor and his team. Firstly, he tells me that I can't wash my hair until Tuesday, that's seven days since the last time I felt clean. I know it's difficult to believe but he then managed to irritate me over the 'medication'. To assist my bladder function, yesterday he instructed me to drink two litres per day of boiled, medicated water.

As a child, I remember catching tadpoles in a glass jar, from the stream close to (step daughter) Tracy and Kirk's wedding venue in Hurst Green. On hot summer days, the jar and its contents would be nicely tepid by the time I'd walked home to show mum. Well that's what the medicated water reminds me of, minus the tadpoles and pond weed.

Never let it be said that Wallis ducks a challenge but I keep waiting for some laughing Jeremy Beadle clone to emerge from behind a door with a hidden camera. Yesterday, I mentioned my preference to fight Ali instead of facing the treatment death crew. Well in an ideal world, my number one wish is to beat several shades of sh*t out of the Beadle clone instead!

Having got that venemous thought off my fast diminishing chest, I will turn my attention to some beautifully crafted manuscripts received yesterday for the next issue of *Cast Metal & Diecasting Times*. I really do know how to live!

Art of communication

Either the death squad is starting to pity me or I'm becoming immune to the pain. We were back to six mechanics in sky blue uniforms for Friday's therapy, most of whom I'd been abused by previously. At least they have started to communicate with me, unlike my venerable doctor and his immediate team.

Apparently, my daily sessions in the glassfibre basting dish will continue for 14 days. My personal oils are reused and changed every three or four days. They appear to use eight half litre bottles, for which I'm charged about £8. You could easily spend that and more on eight hours of high quality deep fat frying oil in the UK. What's more, this stuff is bound to be organic. It also acts as a substitute for Grecian 2000, if the colour of my hair is anything to go by.

Applying the oil must be tiring and mind numbing when it's all you do to people through the day. The session begins with me facing down for 10 minutes, before sliding onto my back for the remainder of the hour. Can you imagine the tedium of applying oil to someone's leg for a full 60 minutes? At least the two closest to your head alternate between torso and arm but the poor two sods at your feet must be bored to tears. Apart from twiddling with five toes, it's the same massage stroke for an hour. No wonder they turn into sadists!

Despite another bad night's sleep, I am beginning to feel fitter and surprisingly, my stomach continues to behave. But I retain this strange sensation of disassociation between brain and left leg, which appears to have little to do with strength or power. It will be interesting to see whether this changes in the coming weeks.

Finally, I managed to generate something more than a monosyllabic answer from the head doctor during morning rounds. I explained about the lack of sleep at night and frequent wee breaks. For some strange reason, he denied my request for medicinal French red wine (worth a try) but bloods have been taken for testing and I'm to provide a urine sample tomorrow. He's very difficult even for me to understand but I think he suggested that my loose bowel is the result of the medicines I'm on. He also confirmed that I will receive treatment other than the basting tray in due course.

The culture and form of medicine may be very different but the attitudes and arrogant approach to customer care adopted are clearly the same for doctors around the world.

Improvements have been made on the internet front. I can now use my laptop and mouse in the internet cafe, rather than being forced to use the filthy equipment used by everyone else.

Otherwise, there's very little else on which to comment. I've finished reading my first book and spent a few minutes before breakfast looking around the hospital gardens. It's very peaceful among the plants, beneath the coconut trees but for some reason, access is allowed only between 05.30 and 09.30 in the morning and 17.30-20.30 every evening. The late monsoon rains have been extremely heavy for the past couple of days, keeping the temperature down and obviating the need for air conditioning. I guess the ambient temperature to be mid-70s.

Improvements through teamwork

I'm finally getting the hang of this baking tray treatment lark. Success in this league is all about teamwork, which has improved considerably in recent days as a result of a consistent selection policy. The two guys in midfield (ie torso and arm massage, plus client communication) have been with me for three consecutive matches now and their experience has been central to the team's fluid passing game in some sticky situations.

Should I decide to recommend them to other prospective European clients, they could be in line for international recognition. I'm hoping to sign them up on long-term contracts but refuse to deal with unregistered massage agents.

I'm also considering approaching Seb Coe for his support in adopting the sport for the 2012 London Olympics. The principle is a bit like bobsleigh crossed with curling but without the ice, hence its natural suitability for the summer games. The skill lies in driving a glassfibre sled-cum-tray down a high speed track, in variable but testing oily conditions. One person sits in the sled, which is generously lubricated inside and out and is propelled forward by six team mates.

Unless he calls immediately for the men in white coats with straightjackets, I'm confident Lord Coe will be enthusiastic, especially if we can confirm Usain Bolt's alleged interest. I foresee a genuine medal prospect for GB, provided we fail to share the sport's rules with entrants from any nations other than India and GB.

At this point, you're probably questioning my sanity which is totally understandable, although I prefer to be considered an eccentric.

Anyway, where was I?

Back to the subject of Saturday's treatment. Having largely the same group of therapists certainly appears to make a difference. In particular, they already know which bits hurt and therefore, how to induce the greatest degree of pain. Interestingly, of the three remaining painful areas, one is the small toe of my right foot, a second the small finger of the right hand. *If only there was such a concept as coincidence, eh?*

The third problem is my right patella, which refuses to sit comfortably on the tray when lying on my stomach, preferring to 'pop' partially from its socket whenever pressure is exerted behind the knee. Perhaps there's also scope for the development of a padded, oil-resistant tray!

This time, I also had a few minutes to discuss the procedure with my tormentors, who are becoming my chums when they're not hurting me. Apparently, the doctor prescribes two oils, one for application to the head, the other for the remainder of the body. This requires separate oil recovery systems and represents a much more understandable concept, almost as sensible as the Olympic Games idea.

As my intelligent and intuitive wife observed, the reason why so much time is spent lying on my back has nothing to do with the application of oil to my chest and stomach. Instead, because mine is a neurological condition, the application of sufficient oil to the scalp via the forehead is of paramount importance. Simple, although why they don't just dunk my head in a bucket I don't know.

I've adopted a more scientific approach to menu choice at dinner, which I take at about 19.00. Placing the list on the table in front of me, I allow the index finger of my left hand to choose but cunningly, without the distracting influence of my eyes. After two meals, the principle is working well, as I've enjoyed both.

I've always been told to work to your strengths and evidently, at least one of my digits knows vegetarian Indian cuisine better than my brain. With training, I'm confident that my other fingers will become equally proficient, although we'll start them on the less complicated breakfast and snack options.

Anyway, there we were, my favourite index finger and I minding our own business at dinner last night and not one, not two but three sets of fellow inmates engaged me (or should that be us?) in conversation... separately! Although they didn't let on, I question whether they simply felt sorry for the increasingly emaciated Caucasian with ridiculously slicked back hair, engaged in another deep conversation about food with his finger.

All of Asian extraction, one elderly married couple from the USA via the UK and Canada are on their second visit. A second gentleman was from Bangladesh and the third, a much younger man from Orpington, does a much more realistic Saarf London accent than me. They "just knew" I was British, although how I don't know, unless my bowler hat and pin striped suit gave the game away.

We must have talked for, oh seconds, before we each melted away into our separate cells, probably to chat again at other meal times. I wonder if they've started talking to themselves as much as me, or is that a particularly British thing? Joking aside, it was reassuring to learn that most people find the first week of treatment hard and incredibly boring. It gets better apparently; I hope they're right!

At this point, I'd appreciate a small round of applause, having exceeded 5000 words of my diary drivel. I am now completely exhausted and will pause to rejuvenate my brain cell.

I now have something to smile at every time I fire up the computer. Jasper (*a handsome Sheltie dog*) now greets me, having downloaded him as a screensaver.

Back on the subject of food, I'm off to lunch in advance of this afternoon's treatment. With limited snacking options, I'll probably go for a toasted vegetable sandwich, which seems to bloat my stomach almost as much as the bread does at home. And all those weeks of avoiding dairy products were in vain too – it's either boiled cow's milk or nothing here.

Bring me solutions not problems

This hackneyed phase is embedded on my mind but for the life of me, I can't remember which pompous 'expert' at dmg drummed it into me or the context in which it was used. Well, I'm all for self-reliance as a means of boosting my ego and in the current environment, there are no others to burden or blame. My challenges may be small "in the bigger picture" but "I'm in the zone" as far as problem solving goes. The fragrant tissue paper and towel acquisitions are examples of recent minor successes, along with a solution to the problem of keeping my pillow dry when a nap is called for post-treatment and my head is oozing sticky gunge. It's simple really and involves the employment of a spare sheet and pillow.

All of which is irrelevant to my train of thought, other than the fact that it's practically impossible to get anything dry here. A happy little man visits me every morning to collect my laundry and returns four hours later with nicely pressed, folded but damp clothes, not quite dripping but close.

I thought about making some sarcastic remark about washing lines and tumble dryers but faced with his enthusiastically smiling face, didn't have the heart. So instead, I set about finding my own solution. There's no point putting the clothes outside on the balcony because it's persistently precipitating at the moment and there's insufficient room to swing the hospital cat, let alone three pairs of briefs, one pair of shorts, a towel, pair of socks and four T shirts. I've seen him or her by the way (the cat, that is) in the manicured garden, eyeing me as prospective prey, despite my emaciated state. No, I haven't stroked or named him/her and obviously, the reason he/she looks so pissed off is because there's only a vegetarian canteen.

So anyway, another, more fiendish plan was required. My cell/room houses two single beds, complete with rectangular wooden frames above for mosquito nets, when required. Yes, I turned my room into a Chinese laundry, draping my smalls from the frames, together with the now soggy spare pillow and sheet. But that's not all. After three hours, the clothes remained just as damp as before I'd started so a bit of tinkering was required. I found that if you turn the air conditioning to full blast, with the ceiling fan running at Spitfire speed, you clothes will be appreciably drier by the following morning, or possibly the morning after that. Now all I need is a solution to the resultant frost bite on my nose!

It was bound happen eventually but as soon as I praise its culinary selection skills, that dodgy digit picks me a wringer, so to speak. Don't get me wrong, the spinach with potato was very tasty but it nearly blew my head off. At just over £1 for the main dish, stuffed nan and fresh pineapple juice, I can't complain too much but if I'm ill overnight, there will be a written warning and if necessary, I'll draft in/on a replacement.

Gradual improvements

Thankfully, my tummy survived the night and consequently, so did the errant finger. I just hope it performs better today.

The results from my blood tests confirm that my sugar levels and not one but three types of cholesterol are OK. To be honest, the printout is unintelligible to me and I couldn't understand half of the doctor's explanation but so long as he's happy, so am I.

Tomorrow I have the joyful experience of providing a urine sample in a pot not much bigger than one for my homeopathic pills. Who's taking the piss now? The doctors again, of course.

I mentioned it the other day but can now confirm that for the first time in nearly four years, the nail on my left big toe is not split. Everyone I speak to – doctors, patients and treatment tormentors – tell me I can expect to see improvements in my condition generally as the month progresses. So far, other than the toe, I'm aware of my greater flexibility generally, the lack of pain in my hips and return to a bony bum. Oh for a comfortable chair!

The gentleman in the room opposite is here with his wife and two children, both under the age of 10. Like most of the UK's Asian population, they are from Harrow and the poor kids look bored out of their skulls. They've been holed up in that room for three weeks, while Dad receives treatment for a disc problem in his back and Mum for some other condition. So I am not the only one straining to get back to Blighty.

This morning, having emailed my latest missive to Joanie, I've been sitting on the balcony, watching a team of construction workers on the hospital's latest expansion project. They seem to have reached the fifth level and are preparing the shuttering to concrete the sixth. As you can imagine, safety is non-existent, with no personal protection equipment. Still if one of them requires treatment for an industrial accident, at least he won't have too far to travel.

They changed the bedding this morning and the gentleman looked horrified by the state of the spare sheet, the one I use to protect my pillow from the oils. As I told him, don't blame me – the oils are prescribed by the doctor, who still won't let me wash my hair. Anyone would think it was his personal sheet!

I have just received refills of the pond/medicated water bottles, pills and potions, together with yet another copy invoice. There must now be almost a tree's worth of paper in my folder, relating to medicines, oils, food and laundry. God knows how many trees it will equate to or cost after four weeks. When I can find the time in my hectic schedule, I really must add it all up.

I am considering cutting my stay at the hospital short by one or two days to see even a little bit of Kerala. It is virtually impossible to leave the site during treatment and one of the doctors suggests that missing two days won't affect the outcome. Because I need to be at the airport between 03.00 and 04.00 on the day of departure, I've pinpointed what looks to be a decent hotel about 25km away that should give me what I need. My original idea of identifying and sourcing local products for UK importation looks impractical but never say never. I won't book anything at the moment but will review the situation in a week or so. Because the rains are likely to continue until October, I'm hopeful that room availability won't be a problem.

If you want to engage fellow patients in conversation here, the best place to do so is clearly the lift. En route to dinner this evening, I had a brief discussion with an eloquent young Asian man from Wales. Maybe it's another Anglo Saxon inhibition but I can't start talking to someone and literally within seconds, ask what's wrong with them. Funnily enough, nobody else seems to share my problem. It's not that I'm disinterested but somehow it doesn't seem polite to engage the trunk so quickly. Anyway, he suffers with rheumatoid arthritis and is becoming something of a regular, both here and at the recently opened sister hospital in Cochin. He's a pharmacist back in Wales and seems to be at odds with his GP about coming here for treatment. He's been seeing some positive results however and is confident I should see the same. Apparently, there were two UK-based MS patients in Cochin last year, both of whom saw positive improvements.

One of the genuine benefits of a vegetarian diet is that when the tummy needs to be emptied as a matter of urgency, it's relatively quick, painless and lacks that unpleasant odour. For the first time since arrival, I chanced a plate of fresh fruit for dessert, a decision that was possibly a tad rash. Pineapple, melon, papaya and banana made a pleasant sweet change but probably not for a second night running.

While I've commented already that there are some really friendly people here, there are others who are less than polite to the masses. One middle aged and sour German woman in particular rules HER roost, has HER table in the canteen and converses exclusively with HER friends, who are equally exclusive. Thankfully, not too many are as rude.

Just get on with it!

Oh the joy of sleeping for six hours in a single night! I may have tossed and turned throughout but at least I didn't rely on the telly or books to get through. My wee sample has been successfully bottled and early morning medications taken, only one sticky syrup finding its way down my shirt.

In total, there are eight different pills and potions, plus the bottles of pond water. At 07.00, I take two of pill A, one pill B and a 10ml measure of syrup C, mixed with 40ml of bottled water. Immediately before lunch, I have 30ml of syrup D and two of capsule E. I hope you're keeping track of the alphabet system because it's the only way I've found that works.

Medications A, B and C are repeated at 17.00, while D and E are taken again before dinner. Finally, a tablespoon of the sticky tar concoction F and capsule G are washed down with a bottle of medicated milk. I have absolutely no idea what I'm taking but like a lemming, I do as instructed and haven't been poorly yet.

It never fails to amaze me how the smallest victory can create such a sense of elation. The doctor confirmed this morning that I can wash my hair every three days. Big deal you may say but trust me, it is after seven days' immersion in sweet smelling Castrol GTX. Having grinned inanely for the last 30 minutes, I now have a difficult decision to make; do I shower immediately for instant gratification or wait until a couple of hours after this afternoon's treatment? I decide on the latter, on the basis that the enjoyment will last longer. It's so exciting, like a child (or Tracy) waiting for Christmas morning!

I try so hard to avoid the predictability of following the same routines but with so little to do every day, it's difficult to avoid. The doctors arrive for morning rounds about 08.15, preceded by the medicines replenishment man at 07.45. I exchange grunts and grins with the cleaner about 09.00, before the medicine man returns with new supplies of bottled pond water. On alternate days, a young female nurse visits to check my blood pressure (with the door fully open), while medicine man comes back a third time with more pills and potions. Oh yes and the laundry man drops in for an exchange of toothy grins some time during the morning.

All of which makes it impossible to leave my room before 11.30. To spice up the mornings, I like to vary the time for breakfast to be delivered, as well as alternating between hot porridge, soggy cornflakes and toast with jam, always served with sweet tea. Surprisingly, it's not the meat that I'm missing but the lack of eggs, whatever the time of day. If you missed the point, I too have resorted to breakfast in my room, for fear of missing one of my many visitors.

I generally stroll to the internet cafe before noon and depending on my need for lunch, either eat something in the canteen or return to my room to prepare for my daily ordeal with the devil's helpers at 13.45. So much pummelling of the stomach makes it essential that I visit the loo as close as possible to the treatment which, if you recall, lasts for 60 minutes. I'm then instructed to rest for an hour, after which I may shower. Thereafter, my time is my own, possibly to walk up the hill into the town or to sit a while in the garden after 17.30, before dinner at any time from 18.30 to 20.30.

Funnily enough, I'm no longer frustrated by my inactivity but try to find different ways of stimulating my brain instead. Sometimes, little bits of work arrive from Modern Media, I read, listen to music and fabricate all sorts of nonsense to write in this diary, as you now realise! From my balcony, I find it very therapeutic to look out over the coconut trees into the distance, especially when the rain lashes down. As sad as it sounds, I enjoy regular one-way conversations with Jasper, who greets me every time I turn on the laptop. I then wish him a pleasant nap whenever I close down. My philosophy is very simple: I'm here voluntarily and for a purpose, so just get on with it!

Tuesday 8th September 2009 will forever hold a special place in my memory. I have just emerged from the most enjoyable and longest shower of my life, having washed my hair three times and immersed myself in a perfect spray of warm water for more than 20 minutes. For the moment at least, everything in the world is good. Tonight, I can sleep with my head on a clean pillow, admittedly still with the scent of oils but clean nonetheless. What's more, I won't have pissed off the laundry man for a change.

I'm now very giddy atop this newly found soap box so my food critic index finger and I are climbing down for dinner and a change of scenery. Good night.

Seamless transition

I wonder what that spooky date 09/09/09 has in store for us today? Despite the clean head of hair, I didn't sleep too well again last night. My sneezing 'allergy', for want of a label, has cranked up a gear in the past 18 hours and is becoming tedious. In addition, minor bouts of pins and needles are evident in my left forearm, having started towards the latter part of yesterday's treatment. I'm feeling a bit tired, weak and unsteady, although nothing like as severely as I am during one of my off-days at home. Before panicking too much about the causes for these symptoms, I'll run the details past the doc this morning.

To their credit, doc and his team showed genuine interest and concern following my experiences in recent hours. They've immediately recommended a change to my treatment today, to a massage using different oils that concentrates more on the body than my head. In addition, there's one change to medication. Doc has this fixation about my urine quality and quantity, asking daily about colour, smell and possible pain. I'm drinking lots of water and apart from frequent tinkle trips, day and night, everything seems in order. If there is a problem, hopefully tests on yesterday's sample will put them on the radar, as only those in the giddy corporate world might suggest (!).

I'm somewhat shocked and bemused following today's treatment. While observing the same principles, the oils and their application were slightly different. Perhaps most importantly, my established team of tormentors has been disbanded, replaced by a keener, more focused and less vocal group. I hope there's an opportunity for a reunion with my old chums. If not, I'll need to create a new team in time to gel for the Olympics.

After my recent comments about the boredom of their jobs, these guys put a different twist on proceedings. There were still six of them, two up top, two on torso/arm duty and two on legs and feet. The difference was that halfway through the session, the torso specialists stopped, stood as if to leave... and swapped roles with the leg men. It was a seamless transition and expertly initiated.

With chin on chest and sideways head movement not encouraged, it's difficult to say for certain what other adjustments were made during the treatment but here's my take on it and as the only one wearing a skimpy nappy at the time, my opinions should count for something. The head dousing routine seemed fairly consistent but possibly with less oil and scalp massage. Instead, it was the basting bath business where the greatest changes were evident. Firstly the new oils seemed much thicker in consistency, were applied warm, initially using sponges and in much larger amounts. Following oil application, the sponges were placed on knees and shoulders, presumably to extract as much residual heat as possible. As the oil became colder, it appeared to be drained off, reheated and reapplied.

This was no longer a common basting dish but a sophisticated shallow deep fat fryer, using copious quantities of Tate & Lyle golden syrup, which I recall vividly from childhood being sold in ornately decorated green tins. The only product that bettered it was the black treacle in similar but red packaging. You never know, perhaps that's my treat for tomorrow.

To the layman (or should that be lying man?), the massage itself seemed deeper and slightly more refined than usual. One of the doctors just checked up on me and confirmed this was the case and that tomorrow, sadly the treacle jars will not be opened specially. Instead, it will be more of the same.

Two hours post-therapy, I'm feeling so much better, less tired and ache-free. I haven't sneezed this afternoon and there's no repeat of the pins and needles. The doctor has confirmed that I have a slight urinary infection, which is being treated with the pond water. Oh goody, I can't wait for my next bottle!

Refreshed by the massage and enforced rest, I decide to attack the hill and explore the town. In truth, by Indian standards, it's more of a village, with no heavy trucks and two main roads that intersect and carry a busy mixture of cars, tut-tuts, motorcycles, bicycles and pedestrians. In time honoured Indian tradition, the combination of vehicles and people is seldom less than four abreast at one time but no one seems concerned.

There aren't too many designer outlets to discover but Kottakkal boasts at least a dozen old fashioned gentlemen's hairdressers, several lottery ticket sales outlets, a tailor and two men sitting cross-legged in their tiny shops, repairing shoes. Cobblers... no they were honestly.

A wander through the village confirms a dearth of estate agents, nail and sun parlours and ladies' hairdressers, so any entrepreneurs looking for expansion opportunities should explore their options. I'm sure introductions can be arranged.

Sports mad locals

It's good to know that England's footballers can win a key match so impressively without me. I'm fascinated that all the pre-match punditry concentrates on the team as if they're locals and almost to the exclusion of every other World Cup qualifier, with the notable exception of Brazil versus Argentina. Sadly, live coverage of the match is non-existent, in spite of being awake through large chunks of the night.

There is blanket coverage of the English Premier League and unsurprisingly, everyone follows Manchester Utd and Arsenal. Glory hunters obviously but great potential revenue sources for replica shirts. Other than football, it's cricket, followed by more cricket, with an extra bit of cricket added for variety. You could easily spend 24 hours every day watching test matches, one day internationals and Twenty 20 tournaments around the world, together with English county matches. India has always been cricket-mad but now, they're positively obsessed. Apart from the live games, there are endless repeats, summaries and previews.

Judging by the state of the remaining paunch, my weight loss seems to have stabilised. I am eating a balanced diet of three meals daily, including more bread and cereals than I would like but averaging once a day. Source of sugar is the sweet tea and freshly made pineapple juice, which I'm convinced features some kind of condensed milk. I am conscious of the need to restrict consumption levels. Equally, I am tiring of the limited menu, which presents virtually the same set of vegetarian ingredients in about 20 different ways.

Where possible, I'm avoiding the spicy options and alternate between different breads (eg nan or chapatti) and rice to accompany. My favourite option is the vegetarian noodles but I can't eat them every day. Don't get me wrong, the food is good but it's like eating a Big Mac twice per day for two weeks... now come to think of it...!

I've just recovered from the most stimulating yet exhausting therapy I can ever recall, not just in Kerala but anywhere. Every inch of me was tingling but afterwards, I simply could not keep my eyes open and slept for more than an hour. I felt completely drained but was buzzing, my strangest experience yet.

Three of the old team were back on duty but I have to admit, at the time the treatment didn't feel as good as yesterday's. I may need to revise my Olympics selection policy. Perhaps they were working to instruction but it was a much deeper massage. At one point, I thought my stomach or intestine was being pushed literally through my kidneys. And when the flannels bearing newly reheated oils were placed on shoulder, arm, chest or knee, I felt positively breathless for a few seconds, as if they were over my nose and mouth. My organs are now feeling tender, while my head is as clear as a bell.

Something has been worrying me for the past couple of days and finally, the mist is clearing. While I've been walking around for a week wearing my greasy hair look, virtually everyone else I see has clean, dry hair. Now either I'm getting better value for money than everyone else or someone's taking the piss! Finally, the paranoia has set in.

My smiling, grunting cleaner just arrived with details of a Kanthakali performance somewhere tomorrow evening on the occasion of Janmashtami. Presumably, this is one of the area's numerous local festivals. According to the note, Rukminuswayanvaram tells the story of how the hidden love of young Princess Rukmini of Kundina towards the Yadava king Krishna "fructifies after passing through movements of mental agony and anguish with the able and timely help of a compassionate Brahmin friend." Somehow, I don't think the cleaner wrote the summary or accompanying synopsis. It sounds like an episode from one of the soaps back home. I'm now intrigued and will need to find out more.

Salubrious surroundings

I estimate that roughly 60% of all inmates are male, unless more females remain in their rooms, unseen and unheard. There seem to be more characters among the women though, most of the men seldom raising their chins from their chests to communicate. For example, the elderly lady from the USA who's here with her husband is constantly smiling and waving greetings, as is her old man by the way. She has a longstanding problem with her shoulder and avoids surgery by regular visits to the hospital.

Another happy soul is a slightly chubby lady from Stanmore, who's obviously on a fitness gig and constantly waddles around the gardens with an infectious grin on her face.

The stern German mentioned the other day looks to have been on her way last night. Her fastidious ways will be missed, especially by the canteen staff. Every time I saw her enter the room, she'd head for a table near the centre, immediately under a ceiling fan. Irrespective of the needs of others, she would demand the fan to be switched off and glower until her requirements were accommodated. No sooner had she completed her meal and moved six paces to the cashier, however, than the fan was back on. Brave man I say but thank goodness there are no sun beds to protect.

I have just returned to my room, following my daily pilgrimage to the internet cafe. The sun is shining and it's very warm. It's frustrating not having the sun on my back but I respect the decision that it's not recommended during treatment. I imagine it must become oppressive in the summer, when air conditioning is essential for foreigners. Having made such a fuss about aircon, ironically I've barely used it since arriving, preferring the ceiling fan instead.

Furthermore, it appears that I have one of the hospital's most sought after rooms, so heaven help those in less luxurious surroundings. I was visited by another elderly patient from the USA today, who had been recommended to reserve this particular room for her husband when he is incarcerated here next January. As chat up lines go to gain access to someone's bedroom, it wasn't bad but because she's probably in her seventies, with crossed eyes and a limp, I thought it was safe to let her look around my pad.

She's already looked at one of the three available suites, the prices for which are "too juicy" for them to pay. Apparently, for roughly £60 a night, you get a ground floor bedroom with separate lounge, bathroom, an en suite therapy room and veranda. In addition to internet access, there's a plasma TV in the lounge. On the downside, they're quite noisy, right by the hospital entrance. What's more, unlike me they probably don't have a wooden dado rail, which my cleaner tells me is the best in the place.

Five of the old team were back in harness this afternoon, so we had a tearful reunion; I supplied the tears, when they delivered the usual pain to my left knee. The energy pumping around me is phenomenal, my entire body invigorated by the experience. This massage was nothing like as deep as yesterday's but I am uncertain whether this is to orders or the fact that the torso guys are less brutal. I discovered however that Chief Dr determines where on my body the hot towels are placed. This intrigues me because the towels are invariably located on my right side, while the MS affects the left. Apparently, the current routines are all about improving blood circulation and it's working.

Not to put too finer point on a more delicate subject but I'm mystified by constantly changing bowel movements. One minute I'm urgently diving for the loo, then it's a period of extreme peace and tranquillity. I'm assured that my body is responding positively to the pills, potions, treatments and dietary changes but I wish it could respond more consistently because false anticipation is definitely bad for my nerves. Anyway, must be going...!

Taking control to the left

I didn't make it to the performance last night, uncertainty about my stomach behaving winning the argument. Probably just as well because I heard everything in the distance and it lasted for more than two hours. Lots of loud drums and crashing symbols and that was just my large intestine. Earlier in the evening, there was a sweet little procession which I caught on camera. A real family occasion, with lots of children in costumes, having a ball.

Without the laptop and occasional morsel of work from MMC, I don't know how I'd fill my days. Despite rationing reading time, I'm already three quarters through book number two of three. Fern Britton's autobiography is a good read but it's simply not bulky enough to last the distance. I'm likely to call on the hospital library for reinforcements and if all else fails, I suppose I'll read what this Ayurvedic stuff is all about.

It was a refreshing sense of achievement when stimulating a minor adjustment to this afternoon's treatment. During the latest doctor's rounds, not with the head honcho I stress, I adopted my most diplomatic tone to enquire why much more attention appeared to be directed to my right side in recent days when the main problems were on my left? Having listened to the mantra about treating the whole body again, I asked why if that's the case, all but one of the hot compresses are consistently placed on the right, apparently as directed by the doctors? "Are they? Well that is because of the problems you have at those points." Having reconfirmed the nature of my condition and its left-sided bias, revised instructions were issued and greater stimulation to my left arm and leg can be noted. Everyone needs to be kept on their toes you know and I'm hoping to get there before the end of the month.

Other than my privates, the only part of me that isn't intentionally covered in oil is my face. So drenched am I in the pungent mixture, however, that I can taste it in my mouth. They've now started wrapping my neck in a towel and once it's cooled, removing it and massaging the throat and chin quite vigorously. In fact, the massage as a whole is becoming more urgent and less like an assisted wallow in a warm mud bath. The only body part that continues to give me problems is the left knee cap, which almost dislocates whenever I'm lying on my front and any pressure is exerted anywhere near it. I need to turn my attention to finding another fiendish solution.

Although it's difficult to make direct comparisons from a hospital environment, there are definitely some major differences between the good people of Kerala and those encountered in other parts of India. This is my first time in the rural South West, where the pace of life is much slower and the people are less frenetic.

Presumably, it's like the difference between Central London and the villages of the Yorkshire Dales 60 years ago. In English, supposedly they share a common second language but speak with a distinct local dialect, which I find very challenging to interpret. Talking to my therapists, there is clearly great pride in being Keralan (if there is such a word) and a dismissiveness (likewise) about those big city folks up north. When I say 'talking' with my therapists, I use the term loosely. Conversations during treatments are frowned upon so the five minutes before and after is as close as I get.

The dress code is certainly more traditional but I don't know if that's through choice or lack of finance. In Mumbai, New Delhi and other cities, an increasing percentage of people you see jostling in the street are wearing Western attire but in Kottakkal, you'd stand out like a sore thumb. The male doctors wear collared shirts, ties, slacks and sandals but most other men still adorn a length of linen, wrapped around their waist and legs, together with an open neck shirt. Every woman I've seen is wearing a sari, mostly fairly dark and drab in colour.

My dress code is dictated by the daily application of oils from head to toe and the mess they make. I'm wearing only a fraction of the clothes brought with me, mostly naff T shirts and shorts, which are washed in the laundry, are worn repeatedly and will be thrown away when I leave. After showering, I'll dress for dinner in a polo shirt and smarter shorts, more to make me feel better than anything else. Why I brought socks with me I do not know!

Business as usual

I remember as a child that Sundays could be so boring. Other than God's house, everything was closed, the telly was lousy and if your mates were out, there was no one around for a game of football. Well it's pretty much the same here, except there's never much to do and everyone prefers watching footie to playing it. If the internet cafe and library were open, you simply couldn't distinguish Sundays from any other day. There's no roast to anticipate, no papers to plough through, no garden lawn to mow or aged aunt to visit. Instead, it's business as usual, observing the same morning rituals, presumably much like being in an open prison.

By comparison, an evening of self-indulgence was definitely called for yesterday. Because post-lunch daily treatments have become more aggressive, I now avoid lunch, which means I'm often ravenous by 19.00. Manchester City versus Arsenal followed by Spurs at home to Ferguson's lot, both live on the box justified a night at home and an Indian meal with my feet up. It's been a tough week here too you know! A portion of Aloo Gobi with Basmati rice, together with a mixed fruit platter and a Thermos of sweet tea is the most I've consumed in more than a week. I also spent 10 pence on half-time treats, a packet of Ritz-type savoury biscuits and I was like a pig in shit. Thankfully, everything stayed where it should for a change as well.

Porridge for breakfast has become a ritual, although the word porridge isn't recognised here. Instead, I order oats with milk, which I consume 20 minutes or so after it's delivered to the room because it's always so damned hot, even for me. I can't cope with the local delicacies early in the day. Appam with stew, Puttu with curry and Idly with chutney and sambar are out of the question and before anyone asks, no I don't know what they are either. In fact, 90% of the menu is both unintelligible and unpronounceable but at least there's no seafood to catch me out.

It beggars belief that after 13 visits to the baking tray, there's anything different to say. The solution to my troublesome knee is worthy of special stage status in the new Olympic event, however, requiring dexterity, balance, poise and considerable stamina. My starting position was on my back today, initiating the swinging rope onto the head routine earlier than normal. After 30 minutes in the sloppy basin, I raised my left shoulder and turned my body onto its side for oiling, keeping my head perfectly still throughout and allowing the head treatment to continue unhindered. Swap to the other side and repeat, before returning to the back, without spilling a drop. The guys seemed quite pleased with my efforts and for once, I didn't swear because a knee cap's popped out for lunch.

The Enforcer rejoined the team today, giving extra weight and power to left-side torso and arm massage. You could see the disappointment in the eyes of the man he replaced, although always the team player, he performed excellent work on the right leg instead. Physically, he reminds me of a former colleague in Delhi, Sanjeev, who would be proud of the comparison with such a dedicated professional.

Breaking curfew

Feeling depressed and thoroughly sorry for myself, I decided that a small excursion was called for this afternoon. The lack of mental stimulation and physical activity is wearing me down, to the point where I can't even be bothered to argue with myself anymore. My third book is boring, there's nothing of interest in the library and I've watched so many Jackie Chan films on the TV that I could cry. I hadn't realised how many truly awful films are released each year and most of them are shown on HBO and Star Movies.

You'll recall that I'm restricted to barracks for at least an hour after my daily treatment so at 15.50 precisely, I set off up the hill once again to explore another part of the town. I know they've warned me to avoid too much sun, dust, pollution etc, etc but unless I break some rules and get away from the hospital for a short while, I will go completely bonkers.

At the top of the hill, I turn left onto the main thoroughfare, in the opposite direction to the route taken the other day. There's a lot more activity here, including a bustling market alongside a bus station, plus plenty more hardware retailers, jewellers and gents hairdressers. All I really want is a nice Starbucks or Costa Coffee, where I can sit outside with a latte and one of those wonderful chocolate twist pastries and simply watch the world go by for an hour. Unsurprisingly, there are no such luxuries, nowhere even to stop and sit a while.

At first I wondered if my fly was at half mast, because the presence of a Caucasian in shorts and T shirt drew a lot of quizzical glances and a few too many smiles or possibly sniggers. The situation didn't feel at all intimidating though, as everyone scuttled about their afternoon business. It's amazing how wrong first impressions can be. After my first walk, I commented that virtually every woman wore a sari but today, the saris must be in the co-operative wash because the favoured outfit was a long tunic with matching trousers. There were also a few Islamic burkas. Most men and boys wore full length trousers, only yours truly looking conspicuous in tailored shorts. In other instances, of course, first impressions can be accurate, as in the case of the naff selection of goods and shops for the discerning or bored foreigner to view.

Nonetheless, thankful for my mini day trip, I treated myself to a cup of sweet tea back at the hospital canteen. It was immediately thereafter that I also treated an assembled audience to my party piece as the village drunk, tripping up a step and greeting the ground as a long-lost friend. Anyone that knows me is aware that I've become quite adept at falling without hurting myself and the best thing to do is to stand clear until the ground tremors stop. Unfortunately, a valiant soul standing next to me hadn't read the script and in his attempt to help, almost wrestled the pair of us over a low railing. Thankfully, he was fine, as was I, despite his best efforts to gouge my right eye. He missed (just), I thanked him profusely for his help, while wishing that his reactions were as slow as a village cricket slip fielder and returned to my room to inspect my wounds. If only there had been a Starbucks!

I was very touched this evening over dinner, when the friendly elderly American couple asked if I was OK, because they hadn't seen me for a couple of days. They were pleased to discover the reason was nothing more sinister than live Premiership footie on the box two nights running.

Brutal is the best word to describe today's treatment. My supposed mate Sanjeev was back on torso and arm duty and he was intent on making a point or two about his massage prowess, mostly in my ribs and stomach. The whole exercise is becoming faster and more forceful, involving piping hot towels and a lot less jollity. Because this was treatment number 14 however, my body is better prepared for the onslaught. Apart from anything else, it gives me something to bitch about every day.

In the knowledge that I'm now planning to leave on 26th September, the doctor confirmed that I will continue with the same treatment for two more days, before moving onto something different. I can't wait.

Testing the patient's patience

Monday's stroll around the town may have broken some Ayurvedic rules but the exercise certainly worked. For the first time since arriving in India, I slept through the night and feel so much better for the experience. Almost nine hours of peaceful, uninterrupted sleep makes such a difference, as does a newly washed scalp. So improved was my mood and physical condition that I had nothing to discuss with the doctors, who were back out the door within 20 seconds!

One thing that surprises me is the apparent lack of irritating bugs and beasties, other than tiny ants that are harmless but everywhere. Birds are equally scarce, the only species on view being pigeons and black crows or similar. While the bugs aren't annoying me, however, I've encountered some humans who've made a pretty decent job of it, disrupting my calm state.

I've been trying to obtain some photographs of Ayurvedic treatments in progress and the patient's patience is being tested for the first time in ages. After lengthy justification, Marketing put me on to the Publications Department, who told me to speak to the Chief Manager for Hospital Administration. Well they didn't actually; instead, I was given a different extension number to call, no name, position or explanation. For all I knew, it could have been my mate the cleaner at the other end of the line. Nonetheless, after explaining three times that a letter outlining my requirements was perhaps a tad OTT because I'm already staying at his hospital for another two weeks, the Head of Bureaucracy, sorry Administration, has agreed to see me later today. I only want their bloody photos because I'm not a contortionist for heaven's sake. I can't exactly take them myself while lying prone in the basting tray!

Having checked in with home via the internet and purchased two Ayurvedic books from the library, I decide to visit the Manager of Hospital Administration to discuss my photographic requirements. Call me suspicious but who wouldn't be intrigued by the fact that immediately before seeing me, he had today's treatment team in his office? In the course of casual banter with the team during my subsequent torture, it seems there had been some confusion over room changes and mislaid patients during the morning. Earlier on the phone, I deemed it helpful to mention my profession and the reasons for my request. I couldn't help wondering whether this had stimulated a team briefing of some sort. If it was the justification, the team members are bloody good liars because there were no signs. And the photos? I have been 'invited' to buy one of the hospital's CDs, where I should find what I need.

The treatment itself passed without incident, although I discovered a few more bits of background information. Apparently, teams are allocated to one floor of rooms, conducting five hour long treatments every day. During the summer, it's too hot for patients and therapists alike. In my case, the head and body treatments each require 1.6 litres of oil and when I explained that people in the UK find it difficult to understand the process, it was reassuring when Sanjeev used the term "cooking in oil".

One of the guys plays drums in the hospital performance troupe and has invited me to see what goes on just across the road at practice. It'll make a change from watching Jackie Chan on the TV that's for sure!

Just across the road was actually half a mile away but no matter, it made an interesting adventure and was good exercise. It was also very humid and is the first time I've sweated this much since arriving. Drummers of all ages were practicing in a wooden hut with large open windows. In a nearby room, four more drummers accompanied dance practise, which really looked punishing for three young men. Can you imagine three early teenage boys in the UK putting in six hours of dance training every day? The troupe comprises more than 40 people and performs about once every month. It was refreshing to witness the different generations working together so well.

Leaving my host to his drums, I retraced my route to the hospital, past two very large swimming pools, where there were children playing and women washing clothes. I also passed an 1800 year old temple and could swear I heard an elephant trumpeting in the distance. Get away from the crowds and into the lush green countryside and it's genuinely tranquil here.

Sense of foreboding

Why is it that some words can immediately create a sense of foreboding? I was feeling quite chipper this morning when the doctor confirmed that my treatment regime will definitely change from Thursday to a different type of massage. He then snuck in the word 'enemas'. After two weeks, I had assumed that the detox was over and that we were moving on to more positive elements of the programme. Instead, doc's menacingly smiling face informed me that a course of medicated enemas would be introduced, so to speak. I am so pleased to have purchased more supplies of '*Exotic perfumed imported facial tissues*' yesterday!

In retrospect, two days ago, I incorrectly used the word brutal to describe my treatment that day. I apologise unreservedly for this crass example of tabloid sensationalism because this afternoon, I discovered the true meaning of brutality. It has taken me an hour and a half to unscramble my brain sufficiently to record the experience, which left me feeling like an overcooked capon. I had been tenderised, broiled and my skin was one fire. Now, I feel more than a little disorientated, in truth completely savaged and knackered.

Only two of the usual team were present, descending on me like a pack of rabid dogs, feverishly attacking for the full 60 minutes. The two brought in for torso puncture/arm extraction are both 60 if they're a day but could those old boys inflict pain.

Apologies for yet another rummage through the memory banks but I can distinctly remember being told off for cracking my knuckles because it was bad for you, leading to arthritis or similar in later years. If this is true, why is one of my tormentors hell-bent on cracking every joint in my right hand's fingers? Pulling the hand away, swearing, sighs, whimpers... none of it makes the slightest difference. He simply smiles and moves on, until the next time he can catch me unaware. Now, because he's been ousted by a pensioner, he's doing the same thing to the toes on my left foot.

Thank heavens for Gloria is all I can say, she who taught me some valuable yoga breathing exercises recently, on which I concentrated throughout the ordeal.

It takes a while but I get there eventually. Now I understand why the rooms are furnished with plastic chairs and other naff furniture, why the walls look filthy and why I can't see the TV screen too well. Everything is covered in a thick layer of oil. It clings to everything and everyone, seeps into your clothes, pillows and mattress, even into this laptop and its keyboard. I'm now sliding in the direction of the shower to remove some of it from my aching limbs.

Losing track of time

Yesterday's treatment really drained my stamina so that by 19.30, I had eaten and was ready for bed. It's so important to stay awake until 22.00 at the earliest, otherwise I'm up half the night. Perhaps my biggest problem is keeping track of the days and giving incorrect details in these notes. Unless I'm mistaken, today is Thursday 17th September and my enema regime begins tomorrow, Friday 18th, not Thursday as stated previously; an extra day's grace, lucky me!

A lady doctor was head honcho this morning. She asked how I was, so I told her that following yesterday's treatment, my rib cage felt like wild cats had been fighting in it all night and showed little sign of stopping. She smiled in the now usual manner, before assuring me that my treatments will change tomorrow, then it will be better.

She confused my addled brain further by telling me my daily treatments were to be brought forward to 10.45 with immediate effect. The time at this point was 10.30, so she wouldn't keep me further and left in a flurry of white coats.

I don't know if I've set a record for the number of consecutive days that one person has been subjected to the same Dhara (head treatment). Every time I'm assisted by a different group of tormentors, they ask me how many days it's been, share mildly puzzled glances before talking among themselves for a couple of minutes. Thankfully, this was the last and the accompanying body massage was nothing like as painful as yesterday.

If I understand correctly, tomorrow we change to a different type of body massage and I now realise why the treatment times have changed as well; to accommodate the wonderful enemas. For the next seven days, they will alternate between Oil and Kashayam enemas, the former after 14.00 on 18th, 20th, 22nd and 24th and the latter at 10.00 on 19th, 21st and 23rd. I can't say that I'm especially looking forward to my subsequent treatments on the odd days. I apologise in advance if toilet humour becomes a central theme in the coming week but I can assure you that enemas will not form the basis of another Olympic idea.

At just over halfway through this adventure, it's time to reflect on the progress made thus far. Last night aside, I'm feeling considerably more energised and need much less sleep. The movement in my joints is significantly improved and possibly as a consequence of losing more weight, I feel more agile. I'm delighted to report increased movement in the toes of my left foot and the split in my left big toe nail is virtually healed. I also have more strength in my left hand but still have difficulty writing. Also, perhaps it's the improved climate but my lower back, hips and left leg ache less than at home.

It's much too early to know whether these represent short- or long-term improvements. Furthermore, I have been doing very little – either physically or mentally – that could compromise my condition. It's true to say that my balance is no better and when I tire during a walk, the left foot still feels only remotely connected to the leg which, in turn, is not fully under control.

Because of the changing treatment regime, I need to adjust the times I work and when I toddle across to the internet cafe to receive and send mail. I don't know how the woman who runs the facility will react to me arriving later in the day; she's already scolded me for being two hours late today. I wouldn't mind but I use my laptop with my mouse and am charged the same as everyone who uses her disgusting keyboards etc; 10 Rupees cash for every 15 minutes. As a leaving present, I'm considering buying her a bucket, some J cloths and a bottle of cleaning fluid. She can buy her own Marigolds.

Changing faces

Having become a hermit in my cave in recent days, I've missed some of the comings and goings among my fellow inmates. The geezer from Orpington escaped yesterday, as did the couple from Harrow with two young children and the elderly American lady with crossed eyes and the limp. It's strange how you don't notice the patient turnover until looking around the canteen and realising that very few faces are recognisable. There are some very sick people here, many of whom leave their rooms only for treatments. Thankfully, most of those I have observed are accompanied, so at least they have someone to complain to when subjected to yet another Jackie Chan film on the TV. Another actor who's made a surprising number of dreadful films in recent years is Jennifer Lopez and I've probably seen most if not all of them by now.

What I've never seen on film is anything quite as bizarre as today's treatment. Like a lamb to the slaughter, I meekly followed the assistant into the same treatment room, with the same basting tray but thankfully, no swinging rope trick. Attired in my nappy, a muslin head scarf was tied around my head and soaked in oil, before I was placed in the tray, on my back and with one assistant at each corner. Having smeared me in oil from neck to toes, they proceeded to rub the oils in using tied white muslin parcels that were similar in size and shape to maracas but minus the accompaniment of Spanish music.

For a while, I thought they were using T-Cut and wax to polish my bodywork because I couldn't understand the need for the buffing cloths. I still can't believe it but the muslin was filled with medicated rice which, soaked in oils, gradually covered my skin in a thick white paste. Having covered the front, the exercise was repeated on my back. It was a totally surreal experience, my head covered in a knotted hankie, a skimpy nappy just about in place and four blokes rubbing mushy rice into my skin with maracas. They obviously think I'm completely bonkers but I just laughed, uncontrollably and for a full couple of minutes. Other than cry, what else can you do in a situation like that?

But that wasn't all. Before the thick, gooey paste dried, each attendant removed his patch using a small white plastic spatula, similar to those used for tiling but without the grooves. Another application of oil, rub down with towels and we were done. Retrospectively, I think the treatment itself was quite relaxing but I was so caught up in the It's a Knockout-type reminiscences that I neglected to pay much attention. I can still hear the incredulous laughter of Stuart Hall in my head.

I'm now back in my room, attempting to prepare myself mentally for this afternoon's fun and games. This morning's treatment was an entertaining distraction from a procedure that has been worrying me for days. My concerns weren't exactly alleviated when the most communicative of the doctors stayed behind after rounds to talk me through the enema process. For the three odd day enemas, she also confirmed the importance of eating a prescribed rice with green dal soup immediately after emptying my bowels and showering. If I don't, my stomach can fill with air and some painful consequences can result. That's a concern for tomorrow but today's oil enema is what's uppermost in my mind, metaphorically speaking. Forty five minutes to relax as much as possible and breathe deeply.

"Oh shit" were the exact words used when the nozzle disappeared where the sun don't shine! If there's a positive, at least the process didn't take longer than a couple of seconds to complete, requiring minimal use of English grammar to find a colon. An hour later, I've done the needful and can now retire to the shower, before communicating all the gory details back home.

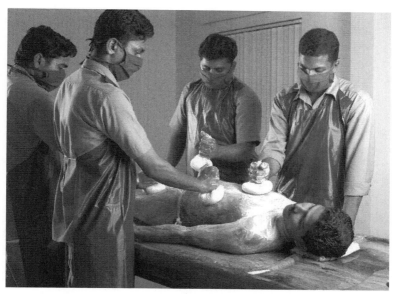

Navarakizhi treatment involves massaging the body with warm and wet boiled Navara rice bags. A genuinely bizarre experience. (Image courtesy of Arya Vaidya Sala Kottakkal.)

Easing the boredom

Jazz is desperate for a pint! He's been at the hospital for five days, supporting his father, part of a close Sikh family from the West Midlands. In his early twenties, Jazz can't wait for his brother to arrive early next week with laptop, radio, anything to ease the boredom. Prior to arrival, they didn't know what to expect, having found the hospital's details on the web as they searched for solutions for Dad's recent stroke.

The friendly pharmacist will also benefit from company next week, as his wife joins him from South Wales for the final half of his stay. He's very supportive, recommending the name and number of an independent Ayurvedic doctor nearby who could provide a slightly different slant on the treatments. Apparently, there are many independents that treat five or six patients at a time, providing treatments and accommodation in their own homes. Judging from his preface to one of the books, however, this is precisely the type of treatment that hospital superintendent, Dr P M Warrier believes gives Ayurvedic medicine a bad name.

Apparently, the Basmati rice polish treatment is specifically intended to stimulate the central nervous system. Yeh, right, OK, like I'm gonna fall for that one again... they've done it again! To be fair, this is a much more relaxing procedure than the deep fat fryer, slopping around in white sludge. If I'm allowed to be picky, perhaps the rice was slightly overcooked and a little more seasoning wouldn't have gone amiss.

For breakfast, in advance of this morning's enema, I was encouraged to eat two biscuits and drink one cup of tea. I feel so lucky. I was edgy enough even before lady doc arrived but when she spent five minutes discussing the impending procedure, the likely outcome and how good it is for me, I wanted to run away. That's two doctors telling me everything will be OK in the space of 20 hours, both totally unconvincing.

To give them their due, the male nurse and junior doc both checked I was OK after the event, confirming there were no pains and the number of movements, as if I had been sitting a music exam. Wait five minutes, they had said, before allowing the movements to take over. When the urge passes, they said, shower and eat the soup and rice that will be delivered to your room. I followed the instructions to the letter. What they failed to warn me was that within minutes of consuming the unpleasant broth and cold rice, my stomach demanded further attention, several more times.

Let's say, it's not something I will do again from choice. Unfortunately, more are planned for the next five days and my bum is already sore. I am both physically and emotionally drained and I don't wish to play this game anymore. Everything is relative but I preferred my torturing chums and the basting tray.

An emotional experience

Whether it was the discomfort caused by the E word or the anguish it created, Saturday afternoon was not much fun. Really tired and lethargic, I cat napped on the bed for several hours, stirring only to visit the loo to relieve a gas-filled stomach. I felt more settled as the day wore on and ordered a meal in my room. Because it's Saturday, I indulge in three consecutive live Premiership football matches, with nothing else to be concerned about except a sore bum.

The following morning, I still feel pretty miserable, concentrating too much on the fact that my balance is much worse. Numerous itchy spots have appeared at the base of my skull and behind the ears but at least my bum is no longer sore. A warning in advance would have been helpful but it's reassuring to discover from one of the doctors that the E word is often as much an emotional experience as it is a physical one. Allegedly, it's very good for me and I am encouraged to persist, consuming as many fluids as possible but sadly not even an unassuming little red wine.

Thankfully, the days are passing quicker, a phenomenon that appears to have little to do with whether I've been active or not. It's the first time I've considered it but there is a deepening sense of isolation, coupled with a desire to see this adventure through to its conclusion as soon as possible. I miss my wife and family more and more as every day passes and I am increasingly looking inwards to find the motivation to continue, rather than relying on stimulation from external influences. Perhaps it's a core element of the rehabilitation process to deal with inner demons, just so long as I avoid becoming morose.

It is extremely difficult to take seriously a treatment that's reliant on Ambosia creamed rice, wrapped in two pound cloth bags. The treatment doesn't seem to be doing much, neither stimulating nor relaxing, the only notable outcome being a reoccurrence of the problem with my left knee. Now I've started sneezing again too as, in truth, are many of the hospital's therapy assistants. The old team no longer exists so presumably, there are baking tray specialists with oils and others with rice; who knows. Rice application has to be a less punishing gig, although equally tedious.

Having been beautifully waxed and polished, it's back to the room for a light lunch, followed by another E word with oil. The oil version is much quicker but it's application is almost as unpleasant as the more penetrative Kashayam E word. I think the male nurse responsible for performing the evil deed knows my opinions only too well. I swear, however, that if he tells me to relax one more time, I'll wrap his frigging hose tightly around his neck!

I'm sure he's very well-meaning but why does he need to enjoy his job so much? And if he should be asphyxiated, who would deliver replacement pills, pastes, syrups, pond water or the newly prescribed cream for my spots? If only he would stop telling me to relax.

While writing these notes, the yapping of some sort of dog could be heard in the distance. After a few minutes and what sounded like gun shots, the yapping stopped. Such a humane society; all they needed to do was threaten the animal with the E word! To put everyone's mind at ease, there were no yelps or cries; I like to believe that he or she has gone elsewhere to irritate others.

Macho moustaches

It seems ridiculous ordering tea via room service, so I traipsed down to the canteen for my morning glass of the sweet brew. Two biscuits and that's breakfast done and dusted for today, as I prepare for another E word after my next rice polish. It actually took me four times longer getting to and from the ground floor canteen than it did to order and drink the tea, thereby justifying the decision of most other patients to stay put in their rooms.

There are two lifts serving the block in which I'm incarcerated. That's more than sufficient under normal circumstances, except at 07.30, when all of the treatment assistants are heading to work on all seven floors, simultaneously. As I wait for one of the lifts, observing the flurry of activity around me, it dawns on me that virtually every other adult male has a moustache. Not a single beard in sight, no five day facial stubble but a phenomenal number of top lip liners. They are worn like badges of honour by the fashion-conscious attendants of Kerala, together with their neatly trimmed hair and smart blue uniforms. Could this be why the town supports so many gents' barbers?

One of the doctors has suggested that if I wish, I need not take the last two E words on Wednesday and Thursday. *If I wish?* If only she knew! Having spent the past four hours recovering from the latest Kashayam experience, I think I will be accepting her generous offer and concluding with a significantly less painful and productive oil enema tomorrow. As sad as it may sound, this is the most positive item of news for days, if not weeks. I may even retain a semblance of a beer blister by the time I return home in eight days.

Celebrate the end of detox

I assume a disturbed night's sleep was the result of yesterday's E word, a sugar overdose or a combination of the two. Justification for the former is easy enough to make, having spent the greater part of 10 hours either on the loo or shuffling to and from it, before food, after and long into the night. Whatever it is they prescribed, it's more effective than dynamite.

The sugar OD is slightly more subtle; feeling a need for comfort food, I ordered a small vacuum flask of Horlicks before bed. The sugar they must have added at the canteen was definitely unnecessary and it certainly kept me buzzing for longer than planned.

Oh what a blessed relief... having explained to the doctors this morning the excessive nature of my 'movements' in the previous 24 hours, the enemas and much of the medication have been stopped. This includes the worst tasting of the syrups but not the pond water. Finally, my detox programme is concluded, simply requiring me to be rice polished every day until my departure on 27th September. Some other medications will be introduced to boost my energy levels, which have definitely been depleted in recent days.

I'm not alone in requiring more energy, as the electricity supply in Kerala is somewhat unreliable. The hospital's back-up generators kick in at least 8-10 times every day, taking my memory back to the uncertain supplies of 20 years ago for much of Asia. It's amazing how much we take consistent energy supplies for granted but how many developing economies still rely on standby generators? The hospital also maintains some solar panels on the roof but these can only generate a fraction of requirements.

It's taken three weeks but finally, I have some proper pads beneath my knees, permitting a more vigorous massage with the heated rice bags while lying on my front. The entire treatment was more urgent and deeper, especially across the throat, top of the chest and stomach. As a consequence, my upper body especially feels more enlivened. A more settled team of attendants has been created and although not as chatty as their predecessors, they're very pleasant. There's only one who I find disturbing; older than the others, with a surly, untrusting look that reminds me a little too much of another former colleague in the UK. Not a thought on which I'll dwell for too long.

Groundhog Day

Another 24 hours without the E word has made all the difference. My head is so much clearer, I'm more stable on my feet and feel more energised generally. My biggest concern now is whether recent activity means my fragrant smelling tissues will run out before Sunday.

The receipt of messages from home represent a valuable source of daily expectation and joy, so separate emails from Joan and Tracy overnight were a major fillip. The pleasure of reading about their daily chores and challenges cannot be underestimated when involved in this unreal situation. In many respects, it has felt like my personal Groundhog Day. Except that now, the conclusion is almost within touching distance, requiring just a little more focus to get there.

Jazz is still waiting for someone to buy him a pint and his brother's arrival has been delayed until the weekend. By that time, Jazz will be in Delhi and pastures new, probably with a large glass of Kingfisher in hand. His Dad is a tall, elderly Sikh, with full grey beard and the broadest Black Country accent this side of Dudley. They thought I'd left but when I explained that I was otherwise engaged for the previous 48 hours, no further details were required, just a grave shake of the head in acknowledgement of a common plight.

Last night's dinner was my first proper outing for three days and once again, my absence had been noted by the elderly American couple. They really seem to be lovely people. Much less approachable to just about everyone are two gentlemen from the very northern extremes of India, Tibet or Mongolia;

take your pick. With their severe Chinese facial characteristics, they both look like they've lost £500 and found Rp500. Just wait until the enema treatments begin boys; then you'll have something to take the smile off your faces!

I've a small confession to make on the bad-for-you food front. Now that my daily pilgrimage to the internet cafe is delayed until late afternoon, I stopped by the canteen on the way back yesterday, for a small glass of tea and half a fried banana. It was all in the cause of experiencing everything listed on the menu you understand and won't become a regular occurrence but it was devilishly good to a man convalescing from the E word.

I hadn't considered post-care medication but the doctor mentioned it today. It sounds like I'll be leaving with a sackful of pills and potions. Presumably, they won't mix too well with European wines and red meat.

Rice rub completed; just four more sessions to go. I am more energised again, my arms in particular feeling lighter and more responsive. When lying in my tray in recent days, I float off to another place, awake but unaware of the time passing. I've become a well-lubricated machine; brain-dead but a good advert for WD40.

Unravelling emotional turmoil

I have been struggling to remain calm and rational about last night's experience since 12.30am, forcing myself to return to sleep instead of writing these notes and in the interim, forgetting some really good phraseology.

It had been a conventional boring evening in cell 604; a spot of dinner, just the one fresh pineapple juice, watch a film on the TV and lights out by 21.30. I awoke alert and ready to face a new day but with tears in my eyes and a dull ache that I recognised in my upper chest and stomach. It was as if I had emerged from a dense, cold fog into a bright sunny day with cloudless skies. The only problem was that it was still the middle of the night.

Joan and Adrian have both emphasised over the years that the process of unravelling my deepest physical and emotional turmoil is like peeling back the layers of an onion. And at 12.30am, that onion felt a great deal smaller. I was wide awake, calm and relaxed. The mild sense of nausea I recognised from times past as acid fluxing, which possibly meant that my dormant hiaiteous hernia was playing up. This was easily pacified with Carbo Veg, a tried and trusted remedy from the homeopathy kit.

The sense of excitement that welled up in me came from the simple act of walking to where the remedy is kept on the other side of the room and extracting it from the vial. I didn't realise until returning to sit on the bed that the actions of my left arm and leg had been completely 'normal'. The fingers of my left hand were working properly, I hadn't walked with a limp, even the piggies of my left foot wriggled. Six hours later, I'm still wriggling my toes as I type. Even though the sensitivity in my left hand isn't quite 100% and the limp has returned, my movements are so much more assertive and confident. I hope this is not simply one of my 'good' days but the start of normality being resumed, if I was ever 'normal'! Only when I engage in anything remotely energetic will it emerge whether my improvement is sustainable.

Senior lady doc was suitably impressed by my new-found toe wiggling expertise and ability to walk without falling over. A demonstration was given, although I decided against the idea of break dancing for the assembled white coats.

All of which provides a link of sorts to another little story I've been meaning to share. A junior male doctor dropped in to check everything was OK the other day. I know he was a junior doctor because he pointed at his unbuttoned white coat and told me so. To be fair, the coat didn't look any different from those worn by his more senior colleagues. For all I knew, he could have been a consultant, a distant relative of the happy laundry chappy or another smiling, grunting cleaner but I've not seen him since. I'll know him again though, by the pungent fragrance of his BO!

No such problems with the bed linen, which is changed every two days, as regular as clockwork. It's always neatly ironed and surprisingly dry, especially when compared to my laundry, which still takes several hours on the air conditioned bed frame to lose its dampness. Even then, the smell remains. My happy laundry chappy will be disappointed to discover that from today, there will be no further business from Room 604 until after 27th September. The oil-enriched clothes I wear between now and then will be left behind, together with my newly acquired towels.

Today's rice polishing assistants were pleased with the progress made by my left toes. Communication is difficult, only one member of the team speaking any English. I have

encountered my first bearded assistant, however, a greying
gentleman with a humour bypass.

Behind closed doors

Mist in the surrounding forests and clearing skies overhead suggests a hot day is in store. I know this only by looking out from my balcony, for I am still unlikely to experience any of the sun's rays personally. Coming from a country with a predominantly dull, grey climate, it's been difficult not to take advantage of the sun. Surely there has to be a balanced compromise somewhere between the benefits of generating vitamin D (or is it E?) and the fact that too much sun drains your energy? I'm still struggling to come to terms with the strict Ayurvedic principles on this subject.

There are probably five or six patients ambling around the gardens on their morning constitutionals but all will be back behind closed doors before the clock strikes 08.00am. It goes to show how little I know about Kerala's climate because 30 minutes later, it's raining more heavily than it has for days!

Porridge has become the central component of my breakfast diet. Boring and predictable it may be but the alternatives are unpalatable. The cornflakes are stale and soggy, while the buttered toast with jam tastes like sickly sweet cardboard. At least with the porridge, I can decide how much unprocessed sugar to add to the steaming bowl. In truth, it is unlikely to figure in my favourite list of meals after Sunday but is probably the main reason for retaining any kind of middle-aged girth.

I guess the canteen takes very few orders for its 'western' menu options. Even though the latest nationality count includes Belgium, Canada, Germany, Spain, the UAE, UK and

USA, the vast majority are either locals or expats from the Indian community. I'm now more of a hermit than ever but have observed four other Caucasians this week and suspect their understanding of Indian lifestyles and Ayurvedic medicine is significantly greater than mine.

Although the treatments have become repetitive and monotonous, at least I haven't been subjected to blood letting and the wonderfully descriptive 'purging'. Based on past experience, I think I'm an excellent purger but it's not something I would willingly repeat. Instead, the dreadful E word aside, every treatment has been conducted on the glassfibre tray: Dhara for the head; Pizhichil oil massages for body; and finally, Navarakkizhi body massages with a medicated rice and oil mixture. Of the three, Pizhichil has definitely been the most painful yet stimulating, while the Dhara was the messiest, needing to be left in my hair for days at a time. My only disappointment is that my symptoms didn't warrant a Fez-type hat being placed on my head and filled with oil; they must have heard about my Tommy Cooper impression and considered it unwise.

It's quite impressive how intuitive the doctors can be. They spotted immediately that I'm weaker and less agile again this morning, even before I had moved from my chair. The process of improvement is expected to be gradual, over several months and not in a straight line. A follow-up prescription will be supplied later today and most of the medication can be sent home by courier. Only minor dietary changes are recommended, specifically the avoidance of red meat and fried foods wherever possible. Interestingly, no reference has ever been made to sugar, caffeine or excess body fat.

Ironically, meat still does not figure highly on my missed list. There are now no genuine cravings, although I am missing access to eggs, cheese, pasta, wine, raspberries and oranges. That list sounds unrealistically healthy for me but it's accurate and complete, apart from the bad-for-you chocolate, ice cream and those chocolate twist pastries from Costa Coffee. I don't intend to become anal about diet, eating only what's 'good for me' all of the time but it will be interesting to discover if my tastes have changed or whether I will revert to type back in the UK.

A challenging experience

My last full day in Kottakkal but I don't think there will be tears shed by either the town's good citizens or me. It has been an intriguing yet challenging experience and every one of the locals encountered has treated me with kindness, generosity and many smiles. I have never felt threatened or uncomfortable and believe their good nature to be more genuine than in most places travelled. It's such a shame that there is a definite language barrier, restricting most conversation to the basic. After four weeks, I know very little about my attendants, their lives and families.

Without wishing to insult my hosts, I still question whether they truly recognise or understand the diversified symptoms of Multiple Sclerosis. Having said that, it took my doctors in the UK a long time to diagnose the condition. Senior lady doctor has certainly treated MS patients before and understands that I have a number of distinct symptoms, each resulting in a specific outcome. Throughout my four week stay, the doctors have addressed many of these physical consequences, notably the loss of strength and sensitivity in limbs and the lack of energy. The medications provided have detoxified my system, while laying a foundation for a healthier dietary regime, should I decide to adopt it.

Bloods and urine have been tested once, while my blood pressure is checked every 48 hours. To the best of my knowledge, everything is OK. I am slightly surprised that my weight hasn't been monitored but perhaps it was decided that I would benefit from losing a few kilos of blubber anyway. I still sneeze violently and need to sit to empty my bladder properly but if that's all I have to contend with, I can cope quite happily.

I have 12 weeks of medication to take home, having cut back from the 16 weeks recommendation. So far, it's cost more than £40 and depending on baggage space, it may need to travel via courier. Compare that to my total food bill for 26 days, which amounts to the astounding figure of £52.

So at the end of 28 fun-filled days, have I recovered from a position of ignorance? Not yet has to be the honest answer but I'm heading in the right direction. I'm definitely more aware of my strengths and weaknesses, as well as being stronger – both mentally and physically - to confront the challenge. In recent days, I have been asked whether I will return to Kottakkal for further treatment. Again, the answer has to be that today, I am undecided. I have been reminded again and again to anticipate a gradual improvement over the coming months and that process will undoubtedly influence my plans. One thing is guaranteed if I do come back however. I will definitely be better prepared the second time around.

A stimulating experience

Saving the best until last, my final treatment was conducted in a different room, with two opening windows and views out over the hills. It was a much larger, lighter room and so much more pleasant. Starting at 07.45, the first treatment of the day, I felt the guys' true strength and energy. The treatment was punishing but boy was it stimulating.

Now, it's a case of resting for an hour, showering, paying the bill and heading off to Calicut for 36 hours, before departing for London. OK, so I cheated by leaving one day and one treatment early but the possibility of soaking in a bath, taking a swim and generally pampering myself before a 17 hour journey was too good to miss. I also received almost £100 back from the hospital, which went some way to paying for my stay at the Kadavu resort.

The hour long taxi ride to Calicut was certainly eventful. Having spent almost four weeks in the relative tranquillity of Kottakkal, I had forgotten how busy, noisy and dusty the other 99.9% of India is. Add to that sharing a 1950s Ambassador car with a seventy plus year old stock car champion and the adrenalin was pumping. I had failed to realise just how far up in the hills I had been. The loud and tank-like taxi chugged its way through forests and villages, around buses, trucks and tuk-tuks with considerable dexterity and mostly in second and third gear. But the driver's toothy grin when I handed over almost £10 for getting me to Calicut in one piece made the previous 60 exciting minutes worthwhile, even though he managed to drop a case on my newly recovered left big toe!

What a difference one hour can make, having relocated to the decadence of the Kadavu Resort & Ayurveda Centre. If my total stay in Kottakkal cost £1000, I estimate the equivalent here would be in excess of £5000. The complex occupies a 10 acre plot on the banks of the River Chaliyar and boasts all the comforts you would expect from a five star hotel. Despite their claims to the contrary, the hotel is nowhere near full. Most guests are either local or from the Middle East. I haven't seen any other Caucasians and staff rumour has it that I'm here for a few days rest from my job in Saudi Arabia; the fools think I'm loaded!

Realising a wish list

Despite failing to obtain a room with a bath, last night's sleep was wonderful. A comfortable mattress was left almost undisturbed, as I slept in virtually the same position for nine glorious hours. The towels here really are fluffy and the loo paper's not bad either.

I have tried to be sensible on the food front since arrival, not wanting to ruin the Ayurvedic effect too soon. Yesterday's lunch comprised penne pasta, three lovely fresh popadoms and one small glass of red wine. My evening meal was equally simple, involving a Florentine pizza, butterscotch ice cream and fresh lime with soda. For complementary breakfast this morning, I've eaten scrambled eggs on toast, grape juice, tea and a small bad-for-you doughnut. That's pretty well everything covered on my earlier wish list and not an ounce of meat in sight.

I'm off to Calicut this afternoon to source material for The Boss and experience the sights, sounds and smells of Calicut. It will then be an early night, in readiness for a 03.00 checkout and departure to the airport. I am so relieved not to be using my stock car racing driver for the longer journey from Kottakkal to the airport at that hideous time of the morning. I wonder if his car even has working lights?

Positive outcome

I was reticent to revisit and update my notes from Kerala for several months. Had my four weeks in India been worthwhile in the long term or would the benefits achieved be lost when back in the UK, living a western lifestyle?

On Tuesday 23rd February 2010, I decided it was time to reopen Pandora's Box and reassess its contents. First and foremost, compared to six months before, my daily energy levels were at least 50% improved. Having recently doubled my weekly workload, effectively to a full-time basis, the energy comparisons were fascinating. I was still working from home but had averaged seven hours, six days per week since Christmas. Previously, concentrating for three hours in front of a computer screen invariably required me to take an hour's afternoon nap to recharge the batteries. I was no longer constantly consumed by fatigue and seldom retired to my bed during the day. A notable exception to this rule was a period of three days in December 2009, having ricked my back getting out of a car.

An hour of massage every week kept me supple and comparatively agile. I still found it challenging to walk a mile or take structured exercise but my balance and touch were much better. Even my handwriting was legible, well almost! More impressive still was the fact that the split in my toe nail had not returned.

The Ayurvedic medications with which I returned from Kerala were still being taken on a daily basis, having been replenished at considerable effort and expense in December.

When they eventually ran out the following month, my system managed to cope quite happily without them.

Possibly the most influential improvement to my condition since returning home came from adjustments made to diet. As a self-confessed former fast food junkie, in the space of six months, I ate a MacDonalds Quarter Pounder with Cheese… but just once! It takes slightly longer to re-educate the brain than the digestive system but when the stomach complains and rejects offending matter, the brain finally takes the hint. I had learnt my lesson with liver and slabs of meat etc, to the point where fast foods and red meat now played an insignificant part in my diet. Chicken and turkey aside, I was more comfortable with vegetarian dishes, avoiding spice and fattening desserts in equal measure.

Admittedly, the menus were fairly boring and predictable but I genuinely no longer craved many of the foods and snacks I previously loved to eat. I still enjoy a glass or two of red wine however, so I hope to avoid turning into a complete food prude! Let me be clear, I am sometimes still bad about certain fried foods, red meat, desserts and sweets etc but the difference is that I now understand the consequences better before I eat them and allow for some recovery time.

Dietary changes aside, I have re-educated the left side of my body to swim again and spend half an hour flapping from one end of the pool to the other as frequently as my workload and continued dislike for exercise permit. In addition, a full body massage (now every six to eight weeks) helps keep the muscles as loose as possible, while aiding joint movement.

I'm sure this more disciplined and focused approach has contributed to the achievement of better energy levels and my ability to work for long hours when absolutely necessary. So too, it should be said, has the ongoing homeopathic support received from Adrian Brito-Babapulle. When I do too much, I am still prone to tire and have been known to fall over for no apparent reason. But then we're all getting older and need to respect our body's limitations sometimes.

When Joanie needed some treatment, an Ayurvedic doctor in nearby Croydon was consulted and subsequently, a 14 night stay at a clinic in Sri Lanka was booked for both of us in June 2010. Thankfully, nowhere near as severe as the Kerala treatments and lifestyle, we were hopeful that the stay would provide a useful therapy top-up. In my case, sadly it didn't, taking me six months to recover some of the improvements I'd previously realised.

Perhaps the doctors took a different approach, prescribed different oils and medicines but my body didn't respond well. In April 2012 therefore, I returned to the AVS hospital in Kottakkal for a further 14 days of detox and treatment, minus the enemas! The treatments and lifestyle are definitely not for everyone but for whatever reason, they seem to work for me. As anticipated, it was much easier to cope during my second visit, both physically and mentally.

Before leaving the UK for Calicut Airport, I remembered to pack toilet rolls, tissues, towels, scruffy T shirts/shorts and most importantly, a sense of humour. Together with an open mind, all were extremely helpful in seeing me through the experience and in managing my symptoms.

I don't claim to understand why my neurological system decided to start destroying itself but I'm grateful that it's no worse than it is and equally grateful to have found a means for improvement that doesn't involve steroids or other debilitating drugs, while providing positive results. I may still be just as ignorant about the causes of MS but I think I've learnt a lot about myself, my strengths and weaknesses and my ability to balance the disparate elements of modern life. Most importantly, if just one other person finds the contents of this memoir helpful, it will have been worth the effort of writing it.

At different times, my stays in Kerala have been – in no particular order - lonely, humiliating, tedious, uncomfortable, boring, frustrating and repetitive. With little to occupy days and nights, it is easy to fall into bouts of self-pity and melancholy but if you already possess these character traits, you are just as likely to exhibit them in Kingston-upon-Thames as Kottakkal.

In addition, however, these retreats also provide a valuable opportunity for quiet reflection and assessment of lifestyle decisions. As such, I have found this process to be quite enlightening about me and what matters to me.

Multiple Sclerosis has forced me to take a long, hard look at myself and to reassess my priorities. Sometimes, it's been a painful experience but ultimately, it's also quite liberating. I compare the condition to a household electrical wiring system, where squirrels have taken residence in the loft and are doing their worst to strip the protective insulation from the wires. As well as calling out a qualified electrician to repair the cables, it's necessary to find a way to secure the loft from future squirrel attacks. I have to remain vigilant that they can't get back in but for now at least, the lights are on and all appliances are working properly.